PRAISE FOR

THE STRESS RECOVERY EFFECT

Some years ago with the assistance of Dr. Nick Hall, the FBI incorporated the strategies described in The Stress Recovery Effect into their innovative program, Law Enforcement Training for Safety and Survival. The program greatly enhanced law enforcement officers' ability to perform optimally under highly stressful circumstances. **These lifesaving concepts are still being taught today by the FBI because they work. Learn and embrace the strategies. They will work for you as well.**

> —PHILIP P. HAYDEN, EdD
> Retired Supervisory Special Agent of the FBI

Stressed out? In this era of change and uncertainty, we all need practical tools to keep our center. The Stress Recovery Effect is **filled with simple effective strategies and down-to-earth tips—your own personal stress-management coach. Read it, use it, and breathe a deep sigh of relief!**

> —JOAN BORYSENKO, PhD
> New York Times bestselling author of *Minding the Body, Mending the Mind*

This is a powerful book that will change your life—if you let it. I worked with Dr. Tibbits on stress recovery, and I can tell you these methods work. **I've used the techniques provided in this book to improve my professional performance.** Sports is 80 percent mental. Winning or losing is often decided by the competitor's ability to control their stress in the moment and recover quickly from it. **Apply these strategies and see the results for yourself!**

> —JARED MEES
> Seven-time grand national champion, American Flat Track Racing

In this seemingly endless COVID pandemic era, the elevation in intense fear and anxiety among peoples of the world has led to overburdened therapists and higher than usual suicide rates. **Hall and Tibbits, using their deep lifelong scholarship and experiences, offer explicit mental, physical, and spiritual exercises to help heal the stressed-out mind and body.** These holistic approaches are field-tested and evidence-based and can lead to reaching one's positive life goals through better health and happiness.

—CHARLES S. MAHAN, MD
Dean and Professor Emeritus, University of South Florida College of Public Health and Former Director, State of Florida Department of Health

You need this book. Inside its covers, you will **find a plethora of practical tools to help you gain back control when stresses run high.** A wealth of information distilled from years of research and teaching. I highly recommend it!

—ALAN NELSON MD
Board Certified, Psychiatry

The Stress Recovery Effect by Nick Hall and Dick Tibbits uses real life examples to improve individual performance. Working with Dick at the racetrack over the years has brought a clearer understanding of what your state of mind and stress level can do to hinder performance. He gives you the tools you need to understand your issues and where you can improve. Simple changes in habit to control what you eat or how you think about a certain situation can make big changes in your output. **Both at the racetrack and in business this book will help you attain peak performance.**

—GARY GRAY
VP – Racing, Technology, Service
Indian Motorcycle Company, Slingshot, Polaris

Stress—according to authors Nick & Dick, we can't live with it and we can't live without it, but we can choose to manage it for healthier and happier lives. They build a compelling case by describing the existing science surrounding the phenomenon of stress and prescribing a priority of engaging the human spirit to guide our decisions and our actions. **Thoughtful, transparent, but never tedious, this book can change your life.**

—TED HAMILTON, MD, MPH
SVP, Chief Mission Integration Officer, AdventHealth

Nick Hall has a SECRET. I first met Nick in 2008, when I was involved with him in developing a Torqeedo electric drive for a Hobie Cat sailing kayak. Or it could have been in 1967, when were both competing in the Baja 1000 off-road race. Nick was on a bicycle and crossed the finish line. I was on a motorcycle and didn't.

Nick has a secret inner strength that has enabled him to compete in extreme endurance challenges, both on land and water, for over fifty years. After reading an early draft of The Stress Recovery Effect, by Nick Hall and Dick Tibbits, I am beginning to understand his secret. He explains how he prepares both his mind and body to deal with STRESS, and he explains how we can also! **Sound, logical tools to understand how stress can affect and even help us. A great read that everyone can benefit from.**

—LARRY SMITH
Founder, Team Scarab Inc. and Kona Concepts LLC
Designer of High-Performance Watercraft

The Stress Recovery Effect is a necessary read for anyone who wants to own their performance. **Dick Tibbits and Nick Hall have captured the behavior patterns necessary to move from good performance...to dominating performance.**

—ROD LAKE
Entrepreneurial Explorer

THE STRESS RECOVERY EFFECT

POWERFUL TOOLS TO REDUCE ANXIETY, STRESS LESS, AND PERFORM YOUR BEST

SIGNS
PUBLISHING®
Established 1885

THE STRESS RECOVERY EFFECT

NICK HALL, PhD
DICK TIBBITS, DMin

WITH TODD A. HILLARD

Medical Disclaimer: The ideas, concepts and opinions expressed in this book are intended to be used for informational purposes only. This book is sold and distributed with the understanding that the authors and publisher are not rendering medical advice of any kind, nor is this book intended to (a) replace competent and licensed professional medical advice from a physician to a patient, or (b) diagnose, prescribe or treat any disease, condition, illness or injury. Readers should seek professional medical advice prior to and during participation in any lifestyle activities suggested in this book and in relation to any questions regarding a medical condition. Readers should not disregard professional medical advice or delay in seeking it because of something they have read in this book. The author and publisher of this work disclaim any and all responsibility to any person or entity for any liability, loss or damage caused or alleged to be caused directly or indirectly as a result of the use, application or interpretation of the material in this book.

Author's Note: This book contains numerous case histories and patient stories. In order to preserve the privacy of the people involved, I have disguised their names, appearances, and aspects of their personal stories so that they are not identifiable. Case histories may also include composite characters.

Proudly published in Australia by
Signs Publishing
Warburton, Victoria.

This book was edited and designed by AdventHealth Press

EDITOR-IN-CHIEF:	Todd Chobotar
MANAGING EDITOR:	Denise Rougeux-Putt
COLLABORATIVE WRITER:	Todd Hillard
INTERNAL PEER REVIEWERS:	Roy Lukman, PhD, Karen Tilstra, PhD
EXTERNAL PEER REVIEWERS:	Francisco "Eddie" Ramirez, MD, Mark Hertling, DBA
COPY EDITOR:	Pamela Nordberg
PHOTOGRAPHY:	Spencer Freeman
COVER DESIGN:	Lucas Art & Design
INTERIOR DESIGN:	Sasquatch Design

Typeset in Chronicle Text 11/15

ISBN (PRINT EDITION) 978 1 922914 58 3
ISBN (EBOOK EDITION) 978 1 922914 59 0
ISBN (AUDIOBOOK EDITION) 978 1 922914 63 7

CONTENTS

FINDING "WHY"

"Dream big. Start small. But, most of all, start.
And...start with 'why.'" — SIMON SINEK[1]

Why did you pick up *this* book, and why are you reading it *now*? We know you just started reading, but we want you to stop right here and think about this: "Why?" Why do you want to read this book at all?

We can't answer that for you. Perhaps you are interested in the science side of life and enjoy finding out more about the astounding design of the human brain and body. Maybe you have a lifelong interest in psychology and in how we think and make critical decisions. Some of you may be researchers wanting to find out what we have to say. Still others may be students or professors, and this text is required reading for a class. Or you may be one of millions of people who experiences overwhelming stress in your life every day.

What is your why? Only you can answer that question, but we do have a few hunches:

- ⊙ Anxiety
- ⊙ Depression
- ⊙ Fatigue
- ⊙ Memory loss
- ⊙ Pain
- ⊙ Emotional eating

- ⊙ Low motivation
- ⊙ Manic activity
- ⊙ Anger
- ⊙ Health issues
- ⊙ Lack of focus
- ⊙ Indecision

That's a good list of possibilities, isn't it? Unmanaged stress can cause every one of those symptoms. Yes, you are probably starting to clarify your why. You can feel it. You know this book is about stress. And you know it's impacting your life in ways you don't like.

- ⊙ Maybe you're working harder and trying to squeeze more into a day ... but run out of hours long before all the work is done.

- ⊙ Maybe leadership keeps raising the bar at work, making it impossible to keep up.

- ⊙ Perhaps someone in your family is sick.

- ⊙ Or there is tension in your marriage.

- ⊙ Perhaps your children are causing you stress.

- ⊙ Or you think you look and feel overweight.

⊙ You have a problem you can't solve.

⊙ You have bills to pay while the credit card is nearly maxed out.

⊙ Or you're suffering from toxic political overload.

Whatever your why might be, it has motivated you to pick up this book, and we are glad you have. No, we may not have experienced your specific *why*, but yes, we know of a better *way* to manage stress.

The two of us, Nick and Dick, met during the genesis of one of the most exciting projects conceived of in the healthcare industry. Looking back now, the project makes perfect sense, but when you're standing on the threshold of something radically new, you may not realize how impactful it can be. Our task: to create a revolutionary wholistic approach to health and healing by building the hospital of the future. The project was a cooperative work by two very different organizations: AdventHealth and Disney. AdventHealth (formerly Florida Hospital) is a leading voice in the area of whole-person health. This network includes more than 50 hospital campuses and hundreds of care sites nationwide. AdventHealth believes that when you feel whole in mind, body, and spirit, you can live your best life. And Disney? Clearly, they are the unprecedented pioneers in experience-based entertainment. The mission of AdventHealth is to create *health*; the mission of Disney is to create *happiness*. Could we possibly blend these two missions into one? Could we create something where health and happiness could exist side by side? Was it possible to create a place where people came as much for improving their overall health as they came for healing a specific illness or disease and were glad to do so? We believed so, and that's when AdventHealth Celebration was conceived.

If AdventHealth and Disney are an unlikely match, so are we. Nick has worked undercover for the US intelligence community, worked with the FBI, and wrestled alligators. Dick is a pastor, counselor, and performance coach to some of the world's top athletes. One of us is a highly respected scientist who spent several decades researching the links between the brain, emotions, and health. The other is a passionate therapist helping people make sense of life and its many twists and turns.

As we began our work with Disney and AdventHealth, we were fully immersed in a current of thought and research and in how to apply all of it to the real world of people's health. As different as different could be, the two of us found that we complemented each other's strengths. Nick understood the emotions and physical responses in the body-mind continuum. He had a core orientation that was comfortable with the holistic notion of body, mind, and spirit. Dick was attracted to the uniqueness of mixing traditional, regulated, sterile, and protocol-oriented healthcare with Disney's highly creative out-of-the-box experiential approach to creating happiness. The dream was a major departure from the traditional approach to medicine. Could we imagine a hospital community where health and happiness permeated the culture in a way that could assist others in dealing with their illness and hardship? We thought so, we dreamed so, we believed so, and both Disney and AdventHealth were willing to dare so.

The first program we co-developed was an integrated program that harnessed the positive power of stress while managing its downside. (This program was the forerunner of what you're getting in this book.) Traditional medicine tends to take a "swallow-this-pill-or-have-this-surgery-and-you'll-be-better" approach. We sought to engage people in their health in more wholistic ways. Of course, we truly set out to do both.

To achieve this goal, we created an innovative community of wellness where health and healing worked side by side. For example, imaging rooms for MRIs or CT scans are normally impersonal, sterile, clinical, and a terrifying experience for many who are already facing the stressors of illness, disease, and an uncertain future. So we created an experience that was actually fun and pleasant. We created a boardwalk, like at an ocean beach, that ushered people in. Instead of providing a cold closet in which to change, we installed swinging doors that led into a beach cabana. The aroma of coconuts and suntan lotion wafted in the air as the sound of waves filled the background. When the guest went into the imaging machine, they didn't lie down on a hard slab; instead they climbed on a surfboard and rode a wave into the tube. The response was tremendous, so when we added more diagnostic materials and equipment, we created a new experience in each room. The strategy was so successful and effective that other hospitals are duplicating it today. We knew people going in for scans were already stressed and anxious.

Going into an impersonal building with sterile, foreboding machinery could only increase fear. We did everything we could to relieve their stress and give them a smile. It worked.

And this was just the beginning of the journey. AdventHealth also specializes in children, so it only made sense to expand the dream into pediatric care. Today, the Walt Disney Pavilion at AdventHealth for Children welcomes children through a lobby filled with interactive characters straight from the minds of Disney Imagineers. The hospital features sounds, colors, and characters designed to draw in the children as if they are featured in the starring role. The Walt Disney Pavilion is the first in the country to feature patient-controlled ambient lighting. So if the patient wants red, the lighting can be red. If he or she wants blue, it can be blue. From their beds, children can choose images from Disney and project them on the wall, giving an immediate sense of control and pleasure. Unable to watch the fireworks in Disney World, the kids can design their own fireworks from computers in their rooms. Every night they can project them onto their walls or send them to other children who are unable to go see the show.

It seems like magic, but Disney and AdventHealth are simply tapping into well-established scientific principles that reduce stressors and promote health. What do you have to learn from us, from Disney and from AdventHealth? The bottom line is this:

The more we seek what is helpful for us, and the more we can understand and make choices that are healthy rather than reactionary, the better our lives can be.

This is the basis of the stress recovery program you will experience in this book. The program does not necessarily control what is happening *outside* your life (though we will talk about that plenty). It starts by taking control of what is happening *inside* your life. We want to empower you internally so you can relate and respond effectively to what's happening outside in our stress-filled world.

We loved our work with Disney and AdventHealth. But dealing with stress is not all fantasy and fun from the "Happiest Place on Earth." Daily struggles are reality. We know all too well how horrifically bad it can be out there, in fact, right in our own back yard. In the wee morning hours of Sunday, June 12, 2016, our hospital was on the front lines of the deadliest mass shooting in US history up to that point. A lone gunman had entered the Pulse nightclub, killing forty-nine people and wounding another fifty-three. As victims were sent into our ERs, shock spread through the communities of Central Florida and around the world. Even months and years after that event, many of the individuals involved have not moved beyond the post-traumatic stress caused by the shocking impact of that night. Their lives are still in horrendous turmoil. And yet some have discovered ways to move on. Some of the first responders that night had been enrolled in our stress recovery program before the massacre occurred. In debriefings, some talked about what they had learned in our stress recovery program and how they applied it in this worst-case scenario, how it helped them survive, and how it helped them heal by utilizing the strategies we taught them—the same strategies we will teach you.

THE STRESS RECOVERY EFFECT

The concepts presented in this book are not simply ideas generated in some ivory tower by scholars isolated from the real world. No, they have been field-tested with thousands of participants in a program we designed. The company-sponsored wellness program, called *The Stress Recovery Effect: Transform Your Stress from Enemy to Ally,* has helped many of the participants.

The first responders to the Pulse nightclub shooting in Orlando were some of the initial ones to be trained in this program. Can you imagine the stress from witnessing firsthand all the carnage a single shooter could create? People lying dead on the street, people injured and crying out in pain, and people scared and just looking for some place safe to hide. We learned so much from these participants as they, like you, faced head-on the daily struggles and stressors of life.

There is a real humanness in how we respond to stressful situations. In that humanness is extreme variation. What is the difference between those who heal and move on and those who do not? The key indicator for those affected by the Pulse shooting seemed to be having an understanding and interpretation of what was happening in their minds and bodies, and then tapping into a series of strategies that allowed them to manage those stressors during and after the event. Whether through individual counseling or group support programs like the one this book is based on, people who understood and managed their stress did better over time than those who simply bottled it all in.

News-grabbing events are one thing. But what about the normal challenges we face every day? A quick perusal of the list below clearly shows that most of us—not only those exposed to horrific situations—experience stress and its symptoms. And it affects us—not only our physical and emotional health, but our work, our families, and our friendships as well. The question is, what can we do about it? Plenty, as we will demonstrate in the coming pages.

According to The American Institute of Stress:

- ⊙ 83% of US workers suffer from work-related stress.

- ⊙ US businesses lose up to $300 billion yearly as a result of workplace stress.

- ⊙ Stress causes around one million workers to miss work every day.

- ⊙ Only 43% of US employees think their employers care about their work-life balance.

- ⊙ Depression leads to $51 billion in costs due to absenteeism and $26 billion in treatment costs.

- ⊙ Work-related stress causes 120,000 deaths and results in $190 billion in healthcare costs yearly.[2]

GETTING REAL

As you read this book, we will challenge you to invest the time and energy to switch around some important things in your life and in your head. What can you expect by the time you close this book? For starters, you're going to get to know us fairly well. We are going to be transparent about our own personal struggles and share with you how all this science and perspective have impacted our lives.

Nick (officially Nicholas R.S. Hall, PhD) is a medical scientist and a professional speaker with a PhD in neuroendocrinology. For more than twenty years he conducted groundbreaking studies linking the mind and body. Prior to launching his research career, he earned his way through college wrestling alligators and milking rattlesnakes at the Black Hills Reptile Gardens in the Black Hills of South Dakota. From working with dangerous reptiles, he discovered firsthand what stress is all about. He then spent two years working for the Office of Naval Research training whales and dolphins as part of a stress-related communications study. Later he led a National Geographic Society–sponsored expedition to the West Indies to determine why whales strand themselves on beaches where they often perish. His research has been published in more than 150 research journals and books. He is also the author of two popular books, *Winning the Stress Challenge* and *I Know What to Do, So Why Don't I Do It?* He has been the recipient of two prestigious Research Scientist Development Awards, which the National Institutes of Health grants to top scientists in the United States. His work has been featured on CBS's *60*

Minutes, the Emmy award–winning program *Healing and the Mind* on PBS, and the BBC's *Nova* series. Until his retirement, Nick was a professor at the University of South Florida College of Nursing and Honors College.

Nick pushes the boundaries of extreme endurance athleticism. In 1967 he became the first person to complete the grueling Baja 1000 off-road race on a bicycle. (That's right; nearly a thousand miles through the Mexican desert on a vintage Raleigh ten-speed.) Nick has pedaled his bicycle more than three thousand miles from Oceanside, California, to St. Augustine, Florida, in one month. More recently, he pedaled from Tampa, Florida, to Toronto, Canada. In 2020 he pedaled from Seattle, Washington, to Tampa to celebrate his seventy-second birthday. During these solo, unsupported rides he has plenty of opportunity to test his stress-management skills!

Dick (officially Richard Martin Tibbits, MDiv, DMin) is a leading motorsport racing trainer. He has coached several racers to achieve back-to-back national championships at the professional level. Dick works with anyone who competes on wheels, including X-game participants, NASCAR drivers, and Supercross and Flat Track motorcycle racers. He has conducted original research in the field of spirituality and health and has presented his work at Harvard Medical School, the Mayo Clinic, the National Institutes of Health, and Stanford University. His book *Forgive to Live* is based on original research he conducted. The book demonstrates how forgiveness is a useful approach to reducing one's risk for heart disease and even reversing the disease itself. *Forgive to Live* has been published in eight languages.

Dick has pastored churches, served as a clinical pastoral educator and a licensed professional clinical counselor, and was the chief people officer and chief operating officer in the Florida Hospital/AdventHealth hospital network. He is an executive coach for hospital administrators and a performance coach to some of the world's premier motorsports racers. He brings to these pages the wisdom of a highly experienced behavioral therapist and the passionate, soft heart of a pastor.

ALL STRESSED OUT

An endless list of factors can trigger your stress response in unhealthy ways. But the truth is worse than that. You may not even be aware that your responses to these triggers (losing sleep, eating the wrong foods, loss of focus, for example) are not only symptoms but can actually increase your stress, revving up a vicious cycle that pushes you to a tipping point. In this world of ever-escalating expectations, the relentless push for productivity and results constantly communicates that "good enough is never good enough." You always must do better, like a hamster cage where you are running faster and faster around the wheel in the cage while seeming to get nowhere. The elusive goal of success keeps you forever searching for something better while never finding it. Whether the aim is to be a winner, to get a promotion, or to find someone who cares about you, *everything* and *everyone* tells you to do more and do it faster and better in order to be more successful.

And what if you are lucky enough to be a parent? Perhaps it's even your full-time work-from-home position. Now that's the life, isn't it? No pressure there. No internal expectations or concerns. Just trying to figure out how to coordinate carpools, how not to step on Legos in the dark, and how to use a belt-sander to get the dried Cheerios off the kitchen table. We all know parenting is perhaps the hardest job in the world. And probably the most important... while also being the least supported and encouraged.

And what is all this stress doing to your body? It has serious effects. Certain types of stress are extremely bad for you: stress-induced dementia, for example, or the impact stress can have on your immune system, longevity, oxidative stress, cancer, coronary heart disease, and the list goes on.

In many instances, the thoughts that occupy your mind are the culprits. "I'll never get out of this cycle" or "I've always been a failure" indicate the *pessimistic-explanatory style* which, ironically, results in these unhealthy beliefs becoming self-fulfilling prophecies. Eventually, you become who you think you are. When you conclude that stress is part of life with little you can do to deal with it, the health consequences permeate every part of the mind and body. But we know from experience, and will demonstrate from the science referenced throughout this book, that many of these thinking patterns can be changed, some by using cognitive-behavioral strategies and others with simple-to-do behaviors such as exercise.

The two of us were greatly inspired by our time working with Disney, AdventHealth, and the AdventHealth Celebration project. Walt Disney said, "First, think. Second, dream. Third, believe. And, finally, dare." We are saying the same thing to you. First, think about your why. Second, dream about how life could be different. Third, be willing to believe that, through scientific principles and some concerted effort on your part, your dream could be realized. And, finally, dare to give it a try with us in the pages ahead.

GOOD DAYS AHEAD

This book is divided into three main sections.

Part 1: Discovering Principles

Most of us have some major misconceptions about stress. We aren't even sure what it is. After reading this book, you will never think about stress the same again. Instead, you will have a simple and clear understanding of how it works. You will take away a handful of principles you can use to make your life better, including a dynamic understanding of "the Optimal Zone," a paradigm you can use to maximize life.

Watch for these three chapters in Part 1:

- ⊙ In the Blink of an Eye

- ⊙ The Good, the Bad, and the Ugly

- ⊙ The Optimal Zone

Part 2: Equipping Strategies

In Part 2 you will learn research-backed strategies for dealing with stress. First, we share Response Strategies you can put into practice *right now* to manage your immediate environment and your responses to it. Second, we will give you

Lifestyle Strategies that make you stronger, more resilient, and much wiser in the *long term*. Along the way, we will deal with *little* factors (annoyances that wear you down over time). We will also deal with the *big* shocks that could take you out in an instant (because you never know when you're going to find yourself in a rapidly failing environment). With some focused practice and dedicated rehearsal, all these strategies will be available to you through the normal daily pressures and in the most extreme situations.

To recap, Part 2 has two sections:

- ⊙ Response Strategies – There will be seven of them to help *in the moment.*

- ⊙ Lifestyle Strategies – You will get another seven strategies that will help *over the long term.*

Part 3: Unleashing the Potential

We will finish off with three final chapters:

- ⊙ Taking Charge

- ⊙ Life in the Pits

- ⊙ Living on Purpose

We're going to tinker with your mind in Part 3, literally. You are designed with a phenomenal biocomputer in your brain. Many important parts are under your control. By understanding a handful of scientifically grounded principles, including the Stress Recovery Effect, you will finish this book well on your way to experiencing a balanced, dynamic life in the Optimal Zone.

In chapter 7 we summarize the most important action points from this entire book into a one-page weekly planner. The plan is simple, doable, within your control—and it's going to work. Skip ahead to The Stress Recovery Action Plan section at the end of the book if you want to get a preview. Between here and there, we will fill in all the details.

To be clear, we are *not* selling you easy answers and quick fixes. You will need to think, and you will need to act. As a result, you will be empowered to find a new calm in the middle of your storms. You'll find more focus in the middle of confusion. You'll find more strength amid your battles. And you might even discover more meaning and purpose. No, we don't have a magic wand to wave that will make all your problems go away. What we do have to offer is a stunning array of research-backed principles you can use to your advantage.

We have worked at the Happiest Place on Earth. We have also lived the nightmare of the Pulse massacre. We think, dream, believe, and dare to say we understand what you are facing. This book is an invitation to embrace and understand your stressors, then learn to work with them (as opposed to either denying them or thinking you can quickly overcome them). As you master the steps, you will find your own pathway to stress recovery. It is possible to manage stress and even learn to use it to your benefit. To do so, though, you too will have to *think, dream, believe,* and *dare.*

You may believe you can't live with stress, but you

will discover you can't live without it. Stress can be found at work, at play, and at home. While some try to avoid it and others become overwhelmed by it, you can learn to manage it better and recover more quickly from any negative effects. The benefits you can expect to receive from such an approach include:

- ⊙ Increased personal vitality
- ⊙ Enhanced health
- ⊙ Improved performance

No need to wallow in the downside of stress anymore. It is time to *go*. Just remember:

- ⊙ Harnessing stress will require some thinking.
- ⊙ One size never fits all.
- ⊙ One formula never fixes everything.
- ⊙ You will need to make choices.
- ⊙ You will need to take action.

And it's going to be worth it. Yes, it is good that you have opened this book because:

Stress can kill you.
But if you understand how it really works,
you can learn to manage its power.
Stress can save your life.

PART 1

DISCOVERING PRINCIPLES

"I am more vulnerable than I thought, but much stronger than I ever imagined."
— SHERYL SANDBERG

Stress: it seems like you can't live with it, but as you will discover, you can't live without it. Stress can be found everywhere you go: at work, at play, and at home. While some try to avoid it and others become overwhelmed by it, we hope you will learn to better manage it and more quickly recover from any negative effects.

First, we will show you that stress is not our enemy. Stress is not the evil that society has made it out to be. Stress has both good and bad facets, depending on how you choose to view it. As Carl Jung once said: "It all depends on how we look at things, and not on how things are in themselves."

We usually focus on the negative aspects of stress because it is causing us pain and we want it to go away. Thus we come to view all stress as bad. But in fact, stress is absolutely necessary for a healthy mind and body. People exercise to stress their bodies to be more fit so under stress (competition) they can perform better. Others take tests that are stressful, which also give them confidence that they have mastered the material.

Some of us may need to add stress to our life while others may need to reduce it. But as you will discover in the coming chapters, all of us can learn to better manage and recover from the stress we experience.

So let's get started!

CHAPTER 1

IN THE BLINK OF AN EYE
Powerful Perspectives On Stress

NICK HALL: OUT OF THE MOUTH OF A GATOR

*I*t was a hot August day in 1965. I was working the most prestigious summer job a teenager could imagine in the Black Hills of South Dakota. I was an alligator wrestler at the Black Hills Reptile Gardens, a tourist attraction specializing at the time in the exotic and the highly dangerous.

Seeing the large crowd that had gathered for the alligator wrestling show, I thought, I'm going to show how tough I am. I'm really going to strut my stuff, all seventeen years and 140 pounds worth! *I decided to take on the largest alligator in the pack: a seven-footer that had mangled the hand of a fellow alligator wrestler just over a week earlier. The routine was to pull a gator from the water, get in front of him, slap him on the nose so he would open his mouth, which blocked his vision, then grab the jaws and swing onto his back. Twice I tried to pull him by the tail out of the water. Each time he spun around to get me;*

this gator would not let me get in front of him. He would take a swipe at me and then dart back to the water.

Teenage Nick's summer job at Black Hills Reptile Gardens, South Dakota

Time for drastic measures.

I had once watched an alligator wrestler from the Seminole Tribe pull an alligator out of the water by the tail and then immediately jump on its back, placing his hands around its neck. I recalled he then moved his hand along the side of the gator's jaw until he could grab and control it. After thinking through every step of the procedure and even mentally rehearsing the sequence I would follow, I thought, Why not try it?

All went well until I slid my hand toward his nostrils. My thumb was sticking up as it passed his eyes. He saw it. And the next thing I knew, my thumb was in his mouth. Thankfully, the thumb was still attached to my body... for the moment at least.

Instinctively, I grabbed his jaw with my free hand, holding it shut so he couldn't try to take a bigger chunk of me. Then I froze in fear and disbelief, stunned by the bizarre predicament

I was in. I was thinking, How stupid is this? I must let go. He can't open his mouth even if he wants to. I'm holding it shut on my own thumb.

A woman in the audience gasped, "I think he's been bitten!" A man sighed, "Nah, it's all part of the show." That made me angry, which was a good thing, because it helped counter the fear-induced, near-frozen state I was in. Their words shook me back to reality, enabling me to devise a plan. Slowly, I slid off the gator's back and knelt next to him so if he went into a spin, I could spin with him. (That's the big risk; alligators spin to rip their food apart.) If he spun with my hand in his mouth... well, I didn't even want to imagine that. I loosened my grip just a little, and his mouth began to open ever so slightly until I had enough clearance to swiftly pull my thumb out. I let go of his jaw and quickly backed off. He proudly trotted off to the water.

Blood was pouring down my hand and wrist and into the sand. I regained some composure, found a rag to wrap my hand, and did the only logical next thing: I retreated to the safety of the snake pit where I milked a rattlesnake with my left hand for the next show.

Soon the swelling started, and the throbbing intensified. Three deep tooth holes pierced my thumb joint. My boss tried to clean the sand out with a toothbrush, but it was clear I would need professional help. So I got on my bicycle and rode fifteen miles to Ellsworth Air Force Base where, as an Air Force brat, I could get a free tetanus shot and properly dress the wounds. (I'm not sure the nurses ever believed my story about being bitten by an alligator in the middle of the Black Hills.)

Throughout the whole episode I remained alert and

focused on what needed to be done to extricate myself from the emergency. I was sitting on the examining table when they came in with the needle. I began to realize the gravity of what had happened. I saw the needle and passed out.

I can't be sure, but I suspect this and other experiences while in a stressful work environment started me toward a career in academics, researching the brain and the impact it has—through stress-related chemicals—on the immune system.

Fast-forward two decades from the alligator incident. It is the early 1980s. Nick has his PhD and is doing research in the then-emerging field of psychoneuroimmunology. He is at an international workshop in Brussels, Belgium. The first and only Nobel Laureate at that time from Belgium, Roger Guillemin, had convened a symposium funded by King Leopold. A diverse group of scientists from around the world were there to discuss how stress might affect the body's immune system.

The first objective was to define stress. The psychologist from Germany said stress is your perceptions and the impact they have on your mood. The cardiologist from Italy stated that stress is increased heart and respiratory rates. The biochemist from Russia insisted stress is the reaction to cortisol and adrenaline released by the body. On and on they debated. These were the global authorities on stress, and they couldn't even agree on a simple definition of their area of expertise. After an hour and a half, the chairman from Amsterdam intervened. "Ladies and gentlemen, stop," he said. "We're never going to agree. Let us just define stress as 'something with multiple dimensions and, therefore, no single definition acceptable to all' and move on!"

Defining the word *stress* continued to be a challenge several decades later. Dr. Richard Lazarus, a respected expert on the subject, defined it this way:

It seems wise to use stress as a generic term for the whole area of problems that includes the stimuli-producing stress reactions, the reactions themselves, and the various intervening processes. It defines a large, complex, amorphous, interdisciplinary area of interest and study.[3]

This is the essence of the struggle to define stress: It can be anything, everything, and anywhere. Consequently, most people feel that "it" is some sort of nebulous force that disrupts our health and throws our life off balance.

OUR DEFINITION OF STRESS

After all the expert debate and international confusion, here is our definition of stress:

"Stress is the tension or pressure between two things."

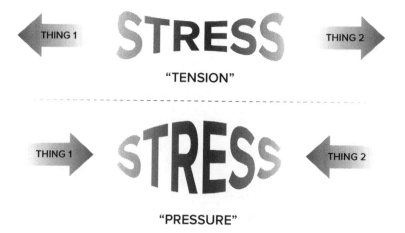

THING 1 — STRESS — THING 2

"TENSION"

THING 1 → STRESS ← THING 2

"PRESSURE"

Let's look at a few examples:

Physical Stress

When a material object is under stress, we are talking about a tension or pressure between molecules. Physical stress can be as grandiose as distant galaxies millions of light years apart as they exert gravitational forces on each other. It can be as minuscule as a single positively charged atom—one of hundreds of trillions in your body—being repelled by another positively charged atom. A common way we consider stress is when building bridges; engineers calculate the stresses the support beams can withstand to allow traffic to pass over safely.

Exercise is another great example of physical stress. Think of it as physical exertion requiring the breakdown of nutrients to provide the energy to sustain it. It is also a form of stress you exert control over. By choosing when to exercise and when to rest, you minimize the emotional baggage that gives rise to psychological stress. Exercise is a form of good or *eustress* stress because of the numerous health benefits derived from regular exercise. At the simplest level, when you exercise you are intentionally stressing your body with the hope that you will increase your strength, endurance, and health. When the workout ends, the tissues impacted will not only recover but will eventually adapt to the higher levels of strain as you engage in longer and more intense training regimens.

During exercise, cells are learning to recover and adapt to stress—not only the tissues directly exposed to the stress of exercise, but all tissues in the body are indirectly exposed to the same physiology and chemistry that arose during the workout. All cells learn to recover and adapt to the stress-induced changes. Eventually, these adaptations enable us to handle future stressors better, including those that may lie outside our immediate control.

Psychological Stress

Your brain is constantly dealing with tension and pressure between your expectations and your perceived reality. (You expected to get to work on time, but you got stuck in traffic. You expected to live a long life, but you received a scary diagnosis from the oncologist.) *Learning* is a psychological stress caused by the tension and pressure between what you know and what you don't know. *Cognitive dissonance* is the pressure or tension caused by two or more pieces of information you believe—but then find out they are incompatible with each other.[4, 5] (For example, you discover character weaknesses in a person you idolize.)

Relational Stress

The people around us can both help us cope with stress and be a source of our stress. Often the same person can be both. In other situations, a person who starts out as a source of comfort and support, over time becomes a source of constant stress. We see this when marriages turn bad, or when someone dies and leaves an inheritance and the family breaks down under the stress of determining what is fair and who gets what. So we come to learn the truth about people: "You can't live with them, and you can't live without them."

The English poet John Donne wrote, "No man is an island." The Bible says, "It is not good for man to be alone." Yet pressure and tension always exist between two or more people. It is often caused by different expectations that cause an invisible nontangible relational pull-and-push. Children in a family or on the playground are always in tension, trying to find out whether they'll get their way or give in and do what the others want.

Spiritual Stress

In the 1600s, Pascal, a famous French philosopher and physicist, wrote about a craving in the soul of a human that we try "in vain to fill with everything." But nothing works "since this infinite abyss can be filled only with an infinite and immutable object; in other words, by God Himself."[6] Is it safe to say that this supernatural tension between God and humans drives us to do something special with our lives?

The examples can go on and on. If we simply define stress as *tension or pressure between two things*, we can apply that to most situations.

STRESSORS CAUSE THE STRESS

A *stressor* is a stimulus that causes the tension and pressure. A stressor can be the psychological pressure you feel when this month's expenses exceed your paycheck. Or maybe it's a dream—a deeply hidden desire that creates a tension between your status quo and where you want to be. So we view stress as something that happens to us. While this is partially true, we can also create our own stress, as we shall see.

Stress is comprised of three parts: the trigger, your interpretation, and the resulting emotional and physiological responses. The event that gives rise to your stress is the trigger. Your interpretation of what happened determines the subsequent emotional and physiological responses. Let's break down these three steps to better understand the process of stress.

The Trigger

We often think of a trigger as something that happens to us. Someone says something to us that makes us feel uncomfortable, or someone does something we don't like. We see other people as triggering our stress. And while this may be true, think of triggers as any potential input from the five senses to the brain, as well as thoughts and memories already in the brain, which have the potential to ignite a stress response. If we stop here, we will view stress as something that happens to us and is often out of our control. Therefore, our stress is someone else's fault, something we simply have to live with. How unfair is that! But we aren't stopping here.

The Interpretation

The *interpretation* of that trigger is the key to determining the amount of stress you will experience. Your interpretation of any event is a highly complex mental analysis of events around you. Your brain is constantly receiving a huge amount of external data from your senses and mixing it with information already stored inside. Like a super-supercomputer, your brain processes the input and then reacts to it as necessary. Potential stress-inducing events are continually being interpreted in your mind. Because we all have had different experiences, lead different lifestyles, and adopt a variety of health-impacting habits, each of us has a unique response to the world around us. Some people will brush off circumstances that another might view as being dangerous. When we perceive danger, the event triggers a stress response. This is an important concept to understand. Many people mistakenly regard the trigger to be the "stress" and set about to deal with it. However, their response to the trigger is more likely to be the cause of their emotional turmoil. Addressing the response to the trigger is equally if not more important than identifying the trigger.

WHAT'S YOUR INTERPRETATION?

Sir Isaac Newton's third law of motion states: *For every action there is an equal and opposite reaction.*[7] This law applies not only in classical physics, but in many situations experienced in everyday life, too. In principle, every stressor causes some sort of stress response. Something pushes? Something else pushes back. When the brain receives a trigger, that information is interpreted, then we react to it either automatically or consciously. Stress responses can be physiological, psychological, relational, emotional, chemical, and so on.

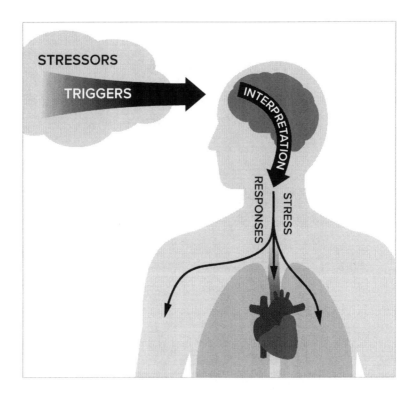

Different people react to the same trigger in different and sometimes even opposite ways. A good way to illustrate *interpretation* is how people react to seeing a snake. Dick ran a summer camp for children, and the nature building there had a snake pit. The sight of the snakes was the same for all campers, but the response would be totally different, depending upon how each child interpreted the snake. For most kids, the snakes would produce a fear response, and these campers would stay as far away as possible. Yet for some, the snakes would elicit a curiosity response, and they would move toward the snakes, even picking them up. This annual summer camp experience demonstrates that the triggers of stress are not universal for everyone and they are not the primary driver of our stress response. Rather, our interpretation of the events around us determines how we will react to any given trigger.

Mixing It Up

This definition of stress—*trigger, interpretation,* and *stress response*—sounds simple. And it is... in theory. In reality, however, the process becomes impressively complicated. Consider that *billions* of neurological actions take place in your brain every *second*. And there are billions of relationships on this planet, each one exerting a differing amount of pressure and tension on every other person in the world.

Reality gets murky because stress responses, in turn, can produce additional reactions. In other words, the stress response becomes a trigger for additional reactions. Your stress response releases chemicals that can give rise to the emotions of anger, fear, sadness, and the like. These emotions can then become triggers that release other chemicals that affect how we interpret a situation. When we perceive that we have a lack of control and are unable to predict, along with reduced optimism that circumstances are going to improve, we enter a state of helplessness whereby we become even more vulnerable to the consequences of stress.

Revisiting our summer camp illustration, when most children see a snake, their fear reaction triggers a whole chain reaction of responses. For example, fear triggers a chemical reaction in the body that causes the heart rate to go up, blood pressure to increase, and breathing to become more rapid and shallow. Digestion starts to shut down, muscles tense, and thoughts become more rapid as more and more chemical messengers pour through the body, affecting the major organs in different ways. You experience all these sensations at the sight of a snake, but you did not consciously do all these things to yourself. These reactions are the natural consequences of fear.

Once this cascade of events starts, changing course seems impossible. But this is precisely what you will learn how to do in this book. *While the cascading processes that are triggered in your body seem outside your control, they can be controlled by the techniques taught in this book.* Join us as we take you through a different way of viewing and experiencing stress.

The Science Behind It: In the Blink of an Eye

According to *The Harvard Database of Useful Biological Numbers,* the blink of an eye lasts between 100 and 400 milliseconds—about one-tenth to one-half second.[8] When an external stressor activates your fight-or-flight stress response, an amazing series of events takes place during that fraction of time.

1. The process starts when the amygdala (an area of the brain responsible for emotional processing of external inputs) computes something unusual from your senses.

   ⊙ A shadow moves outside your bedroom window.

   ⊙ A fire alarm goes off.

⊙ Sirens blare behind you in traffic.

⊙ You realize your child is missing.

⊙ You hear a gunshot.

⊙ Your spouse screams.

⊙ You find your thumb in an alligator's mouth.

⊙ An eighteen-wheeler jackknifes in front of you. (Spoiler alert: This happens to one of us at the end of the chapter.)

2. The amygdala and other brain structures send an alarm message to the hypothalamus (a portion of the brain that acts like a war room command center). The hypothalamus ignites the release of neurotransmitters that trigger a number of physiological changes that help the body and brain respond to the perceived danger.

⊙ Sight, hearing, and other senses become sharper.

⊙ Conscious thought slows, and reflexes kick in.

⊙ Blood is directed away from the skin and internal organs to the heart, lungs, and

muscles needed for the fight-or-flight
survival response.

⊙ Heart rate and strength of contraction of
the heart increase to augment blood flow
as much as 400%.

⊙ Blood sugar (glucose) and fats are released
from temporary storage sites. These
nutrients flood into the bloodstream,
supplying energy to all parts of the body.

⊙ Blood that supplies required oxygen
and glucose to the muscles and brain is
increased.

⊙ Small airways in the lungs open wide,
allowing the lungs to take in as much
oxygen as possible with each breath.

⊙ Breathing rates go up to supply necessary
oxygen to the heart, brain, and exercising
muscle.

⊙ Oxygen is transported by red blood cells to
increase metabolism, while the immune
system is mobilized to ward off infections.

⊙ Extra oxygen is sent to the brain,
increasing alertness.

⊙ The spleen discharges red and white blood cells, allowing the blood to transport more oxygen and provide protection in case you get bitten or stabbed during a battle.

⊙ Sweat production increases to release excess heat and maintain body temperature.

⊙ Blood thickens as platelets prepare to stop impending bleeding.

⊙ Production of digestive secretions is severely reduced.

These changes happen so quickly we don't even know they're happening. When something startles you, the body's wiring is so efficient that the amygdala and hypothalamus (which in turn receive input directly or indirectly from throughout the brain) ignite these stress reactions even before the brain's cognitive centers have had a chance to fully process what is happening.

3. After a second or so, the initial surge of chemicals subsides. But if the amygdala is still sending warning signals, the hypothalamus activates a second part of the stress response system, the hypothalamic-pituitary-adrenal (HPA) axis, a brain network consisting of the

hypothalamus, the pituitary gland, and the adrenal glands.

⊙ The hypothalamus releases corticotropin-releasing hormone (CRH), which rushes to the pituitary gland.

⊙ The pituitary gland triggers the release of adrenocorticotropic hormone (ACTH).

⊙ ACTH travels through the bloodstream to the adrenal glands, prompting them to release cortisol. Cortisol is the main stress hormone that we produce in the wake of nearly any perceived threat. Its job is to provide energy when you need extra glucose in your bloodstream. Indeed, cortisol helps provide the energy to keep the whole body revved up and on high alert.

⊙ When the threat passes, cortisol levels fall, and the parasympathetic nervous system puts the brakes on the stress response. And everything returns to normal.

Many books have been written on the topic of stress. Genetics is the foundation of who we are and what we do, including the stress response. Our foundation is also the experiences we have as children, the events that happened to Mom when she was pregnant, our nutrition, exposure to environmental toxins, whether we grew up rich or poor, our gender, treatment by others, and so on. Nothing is simple when trying to understand behavior, and we don't want to convey the impression that it is. But despite the complexity, some simple strategies exist that we will soon describe for maintaining an even keel when stress causes us to start unraveling at the seams.[9]

STRESS IS NOT A FOUR-LETTER WORD

Stress is a universal phenomenon. Properly understood, stress is not just part of life; it *is* life—a dynamic that is inseparable from our existence. The most common understanding of stress is that it is always bad and we have way too much of it. Let's throw out that assumption. That's simply the wrong way to view it. Stressors aren't bad. But stressors aren't inherently good, either. Even exercise—a stressor that can have tremendous benefits for the body, soul, and spirit—can turn against you when you have too much or too little in a given situation.

The bottom line: You want to change your view of stress as always being *bad* and rather view stress as always having the potential to be either *good* or *bad* for you, depending on how you manage it.

Life is filled with tension and pressure at *every* level: molecular, social, cultural, financial, nutritional, and so on. Innumerable tensions and pressures put our lives in constant, complicated, and dynamic balance. We are continually under pressure and tension. We can't live without them. Consider actions you do all the time. You get out of bed. Lean over to tie your shoes. Watch the news. Walk up the stairs. Even small actions cause tension and pressure that trigger stress responses. Stressors shouldn't be labeled as "good" or "bad." Instead, the way we evaluate, label, and respond to them defines them... and us.

IDENTIFYING YOUR STRESS-COPING STYLE

It all boils down to the fact that we each have our own stress-coping style. For some, that style can even shape our personality. There is the type A coping style where the individual is impatient and competitive and may even have an edge of hostility about them.[10] Their approach can amplify stress for them and create stress for others. On the other end of the spectrum is the type C style that tends to look outward for approval and seeks not to disappoint. This individual often copes with stress by seeking to avoid it, which only causes stress to build up more with time.[11]

Our view of the world impacts how we respond to stressors. The optimist looks for the good in situations, and the pessimist is sure things will only get worse. The socially isolated often lack helpful perspectives from others, while the socialite rarely goes below the surface to understand the deeper underlying forces at work in their life. Depression, hostility, anxiety, learned hopelessness, and a whole range of personality factors all contribute to your unique coping style.

You probably can't imagine going at speeds over one hundred miles per hour just inches away from another vehicle (on slippery dirt, to boot) or launching yourself forty feet in the air. The motorcycle racers Dick coaches do it all the time.

Kevin Windham was one of the most naturally talented riders
in Supercross history (Credit: Spencer Freeman)

Dick and Kevin exchanging ideas between races (Credit: Spencer Freeman)

Jared Mees, Seven-Time Grand National Flat Track Champion
(Credit: Dave Hoenig, Flat Trak Fotos)

Dick celebrating one of Jared's many race wins with him
(Credit: Dave Hoenig, Flat Trak Fotos)

Supercross riders are subjected to huge pressures and tensions. Thousands of dollars of prize and sponsorship money ride on fractions of seconds. One little slip can mean serious injury or even death—and yet the riders seek this stress each day. Even for the pros, there's a tipping point where the stressors no longer serve a useful purpose but in fact work against them. Too few stressors and they will not be able to perform at their peak; too many stressors and they will start falling back in the pack. Where is this tipping point? Determining that is as much an art as a science. The principles of stress recovery play a huge part in this determination (more on that in Part 3). Harnessing the scientific principles of stress recovery can enable you to handle more stressors than ever before. Furthermore, some of the stress issues we face come from having too little, rather than too much. Strategically introducing stressors into key areas of your life brings vitality, healing, health, and power (more on that in Part 2).

No, stress is not a four-letter word. It's not simply a *part* of life. It *is* life on all levels. It keeps everything in the physical world moving. It's the glue that keeps a marriage alive. It's the inner yearning that keeps us hungry for deeper purpose and a higher power.

Erase those false notions about stress being bad. Embrace a new paradigm you can use to manage your stress triggers, interpretations, and stress responses with scientific principles you can use to make your life better! If you dig deep and think hard, you will continue to discover that stress can even bring a stunning depth of purpose and meaning to life. And we tell you that from experience.

DICK TIBBITS: CRASH COURSE

It was December 23, 1968, around midnight when I slid the key into the ignition of my family's old station wagon. Honestly, I resented that car. All my friends were driving the muscle cars from the '60s, with cool chrome trim and massive V8s. I remember telling Dad, "I wish an accident would destroy this thing so we could get a real car."

My dad, who had dropped out of school to work through the Depression, was struggling night and day to keep our family fed via his Harley motorcycle shop... those years were not the "good ol' days" for Harley Davidson. Me? I was a hard-charging teen in the social scene and on the athletic field. I did whatever it took to win. I did everything 100 percent.

That winter night, my friends and I had been out celebrating around the holiday season. As the festivities wound down, I started the old station wagon and pulled onto the snow-packed, two-lane road toward home. Just a normal night for a teen... until a few miles down, in the blink of an eye, an oncoming eighteen-wheeler slammed on his brakes, jackknifed on the frozen highway, and slid head-on into me.

Many people who are under intense stressors eventually feel like giving up. It can take a long time to reach this despair. For me, the whole stress dimension of intensity—going from frustrated to distressed to overwhelmed to giving up—all was condensed into a moment. I felt helpless and powerless. I had no options to get out.

I'm dead, I thought. With that notion I grabbed on to the steering wheel and just held tight.

Then everything went black.

Reality returned in blurry snapshots: I see the people pulling me out of the passenger side. I see the semitruck embedded in the front end of my car. Then I black out again. In the next picture I am sitting on the front porch of someone's house. They are wiping blood from my face and telling me my parents are on the way. Everything goes black again. Next, my mom, a nurse, is shaving my head in a doctor's office, applying butterfly bandages to my scalp and dressing my bloody knees.

The next day we went to the lot where my car had been towed. Silence ensued as we surveyed the twisted pile of metal. The hood had sliced through the windshield, cut off the steering wheel, and was embedded deep into the driver's seat—precisely where my shoulders and neck should have been.

How had it missed me? I don't know. There's no explanation for how I could have been pushed down so low that the hood didn't take my head. As I stood surveying the wreckage, I couldn't escape the thought that this was a very real miracle.

I could have died. What did all this mean?

Restless questions began gnawing at my heart.

- ⊙ *Where do I go from here?*

- ⊙ *What am I doing with my life?*

- ⊙ *What is the meaning of life?*

- ⊙ *What was the purpose of this accident?*

- ⊙ *What is MY purpose ... ?*

My search for answers was earnest and led to the beginning of my spiritual journey. This inner transformation changed my life. I went from not caring to embracing life fully. If your life has purpose, you WILL have motivation. From barely surviving high school, I went on to college and grad school, got married, and had a child and a successful career.

I'll never forget that moment in time that changed my life; it was a death and a rebirth in a very real way. Looking back, stressors and stress responses had everything to do with the story.

Physiologically, my body's response to the physical trauma saved my life. I can't tell you what my heart rate was. I'm sure it was off the chart. When under acute stressors, our bodies release hormones into our systems that protect us and preserve us in every way, even numbing our senses to get us through traumatic shock.

Psychologically, the stress forced me to consider the reality of my mortality. It was a dark time; yet there is a light in every storm. I can either be defeated, or I can find purpose in what's happening to me. If you believe all things work together for good and all things can have a purpose, then you start assessing, what can I learn from this?

Spiritually, the stressors created an awareness of a healthy tension between me and God. People can go through horrendous situations and come out stronger because, in that situation, they find a purpose in life. Our difficult places can become a source of strength for us; our past struggles can provide a source of help for those going through similar circumstances. Because of our struggles we can become "wounded healers" for others. So it is true: the stressors in our lives can be good or bad. Circumstances don't determine the course of our lives, but rather our response to the circumstances we are dealt determine it.

While this happened a long time ago, who I am today is a result of that moment in time. That moment radically redirected my life, although it was an event over which I had no control. I couldn't control the situation, but I could choose how to respond. I could just as easily have gotten depressed and thrown my life away. A best friend in high school faced intense stressors when his older brother was killed in a car accident. I can remember him drinking himself almost to death.

The impact of two separate car accidents took two different people in two different directions. My friend said, regarding his experience, "Life isn't fair. What difference does it make?" I considered my experience and said, "Life must have meaning and purpose. There must be more to life than this."

Stress is simply a reminder that we have life choices to

make. Are we going to let the stress overwhelm us, or are we going to recover? Are we going to move on to a better place? It took a near-fatal accident to teach me that lesson.

TAKE A DEEP BREATH!

We have covered a lot of ground in this chapter. By defining, in practical terms, *stress, stressors, triggers, interpretations,* and *stress responses*, we are ready to examine some of the scientifically based action points to make life better. Interestingly, some conventional wisdom is wise too. Grandma knew a thing or two about stress recovery strategies long ago. It just took science a while to catch up.

- Take a time out.

- Take a nap.

- Take a shower.

- Go for a walk.

- Go out and play.

- Take time to pray about it.

- Or just sit back in a rocking chair and rock your troubles away.

All of that is sound advice. We are setting the stage for the practical strategies packed into Part 2. But why wait? There's one strategy you can do right now, right where you are, to begin managing your stress response.

Grandma had good reason to tell you to "take a deep breath" when you were exhibiting an "inappropriate stress response," for example, screaming and crying when you didn't know what else to do. Taking a long, slow, deep breath is a multipurpose Stress Recovery Strategy that:

- Cools your brain if you inhale through your nostrils
- Improves oxygen flow
- Relaxes your tension
- Gives you a moment to think

Try It:

- Sit up straight or lie down if possible.
- Put your hands to your sides or rest them on your thighs.
- Breathe in through your nose and out through your mouth. This helps adjust the temperature of the incoming air to that of your lungs.
- When you inhale, imagine your stomach to be a balloon you are blowing up until full. You can even put your hands gently on your stomach to feel it rise and fall.
- While extending your stomach outward, fill your chest and then expand all the way up to your shoulders.

⊙ Hold the breath for a count of three.

⊙ Then let it all out slowly. Your exhale should be about one-third longer than your inhale. The reason for this is that the maximum relaxation occurs on the exhale.

⊙ Repeat three to five times.

⊙ And then get ready for much more in chapter 2.

Important Note: Throughout this book we will suggest many applications that involve physical exertion. Prior to engaging in any of these exercises, we recommend you consult with your physician, especially if you have any condition that make these activities risky or if you have not exercised regularly in the past. If you ever feel chest pain or dizziness, or pressure in your chest while increasing your heart rate, stop the exercise immediately and be checked by a physician as soon as possible.

CHAPTER 1 TAKEAWAYS

Lesson from a Gator

Stress happens. Sometimes it happens because of hormone-driven adolescent imprudence. Regardless of the reason, our bodies and brains are designed to respond to it, and we can learn and grow from it.

Definitions:

- ⊙ **Stress** is a tension or pressure between two things. Some of the different kinds of stress include physical, psychological, and spiritual.

- ⊙ **Stressors** activate the senses and create the tension. The intensity and impact of stressors are highly relative to the situation and the person.

- ⊙ **Triggers** are inputs from the five senses to the brain, as well as thoughts and memories already in the brain.

- ⊙ **Interpretation** is the highly complex mental analysis of triggers. Because every human brain is unique and contains the memories of different experiences, our interpretations of a variety of triggers—and, therefore, our reactions to those triggers—vary from person to person and situation to situation.

⊙ **Stress Responses** arise according to the brain's interpretation of the triggers. For every action there will be an equal and opposite reaction. Learning to manage stressors using an equal and opposite response will change your life for the better.

In the Blink of an Eye: How the Process Is Designed to Work

The human body has intricate systems designed to save your life when you encounter dangerous acute stressors. Understanding something about those systems helps us appreciate them when we need them.

Stress Is Not a Four-Letter Word

A broad definition of stress reveals that stressors aren't inherently good or bad. Learning to *manage* stressors and *respond* to them appropriately is the key to improved *recovery* from their consequences. This involves a basic understanding of how triggers and interpretations work.

Dick Tibbits's "Crash Course"

Sometimes it takes a hard jolt of stressors to get us thinking about the most important considerations in life... and beyond.

Take a Deep Breath!

Breathe in slowly, pause a second, hold your breath, and then breathe out even slower than you breathed in.

CHAPTER 2

THE GOOD, THE BAD, AND THE UGLY

The Essential Paradigm Shift

DICK TIBBITS: NOT EVEN A PINK SLIP, PART 1

*A*t first, his words weren't registering in my brain. I could see his mouth moving; I could hear the sounds coming out, but what he was saying just didn't translate into anything I was expecting.

This man was my friend. Sure, he was my boss, but we had walked through some very difficult times together. We had also played tennis together every week. I was a high performer who was known for getting things done. I'd been with this company for ten years—eight of those spent working arm-in-arm with my friend.

But when I walked into his office that morning, he didn't stand up to greet me. He didn't make eye contact. He simply said, "Have a seat." And then he started to read from a script.

"As a result of the reengineering we are going through to

improve productivity and to lower our cost of doing business...
[and] as a result of the recommendations made by our consultants
around what the organization should look like going forward...
your position has been eliminated." His words then drifted
off into something about how much all my work and efforts
were appreciated, and don't forget to pick up all your personal
belongings on your way out the door.

I interrupted, "I don't understand. What are you saying?"

He started reading the script again and got about halfway
through.

"Stop," I interrupted again. "Are you telling me that I'm
fired?"

"You're not being fired. You're being reengineered."

In the moment (and still today), I saw no practical difference
between the words "fired" and "reengineered." Perhaps it made a
difference to some employee relations expert someplace, but the
distinction didn't make sense to me. His final words did make
sense, however: "You need to pack your things and leave the
building. If you're gone within the next hour, that's best."

That was it.

I was given a few minutes to load up my personal belongings
in a box and turn in my badge. No two-week notice. No thank-
you party. No goodbyes. Not even a pink slip.

I was simply to disappear.

I drove home in a mental and emotional fog. When I walked
into my home, everything felt out of place, including me. What
am I doing here on a weekday morning? *My whole existence*
was suspended in surreal numbness.

How do I tell my family? *At dinner, dazed and in disbelief,*

the words tumbled out to my wife and daughter. "Reengineering...
Fired... No more paycheck..."

I was a textbook case of shock and denial (the first two
stages of grief after a traumatic loss, according to Dr. Elisabeth
Kübler-Ross). My wife, on the other hand, had no problems
properly interpreting the words. She jumped over the first two
stages and went right into anger. "How could they? After all you
have done! Just like that? What are we going to do?" I probably
uttered some hollow clichés of Christian comfort: "God is in
control; He will work everything out just fine." Then I went to
bed still in a fog.

The next morning the fog lifted. As I sat alone in the empty
house, denial was engulfed in a swirling dark cloud of thoughts
and emotions billowing in my brain. Slowly, the brutal clarity of
reality set in.

My wife had just started her master's degree. My daughter
was going to college. How would we pay for that? This was
absolutely unfair. After all I had done for the company, after
all the sweat and tears I had poured into my work. Being let
go was unjust, really. Morally wrong. I had given my all. I had
done nothing wrong. I had excelled above and beyond—and yet
I had been disposed of, thrown out, coldly, heartlessly. I felt like
unwanted trash left by the side of the curb, waiting to be dumped
and taken away! I felt... betrayed.

That sense of betrayal was probably the most intense
mental stressor of all. The emotion was pervasive. Over the
following days and weeks, the billowing clouds of dark thoughts
transformed into a raging thunderstorm. I gritted my teeth as the
anger flashed like lightning. I vowed I would never be vulnerable

again like that. I would not work for another company that could simply throw me away like yesterday's news.

Since most of my life revolved around work, I wasn't sure what to do with myself. Even my friends, who were largely people I worked with, felt awkward around me. Not knowing what to say, they simply stopped being around me.

I also quit exercising since even that activity had been built around my work. No one to play tennis with. I ate whatever I felt like—which was almost always the wrong food. As a result, I put on weight. I was feeling heavy emotionally as well as physically. Sitting on the couch watching TV soon become my life, which was interrupted only by the commercials.

People could see I was no longer myself, at least not the person I had always been. Some tried to help. They would offer advice like, "Pull yourself together" or "Get over it." But I didn't know how. I was consumed with repeatedly rehashing the events that had happened, only to realize I couldn't have done anything to change them. I felt powerless and victimized.

Weeks slipped by in a haze of rogue emotions. As weeks turned into months, chronic stress symptoms began to appear. My blood pressure was up, I was feeling tired all the time, and I started to get nagging headaches. My doctor watched this steady decline in my health and mental well-being. But he had little advice to offer, and when you're depressed, you don't have the initiative to do anything anyway. In the darkest hours I simply did not care what would happen. That scared my wife and my daughter, who were depending on me to help support them through their educational pursuits.

And spiritually? Who wants to go to church when you're in a state like that? I had, after all, been fired from a faith-based organization. Why would I want to get back into religion and set myself up for more rejection and pain? Soon a deeper, soul-disturbing question began shouting into my darkness: Wasn't God really the one at fault for all of this? At the least, why didn't He prevent it from happening?

Though I was unable to recognize it at the time, the acute stress response—so beautifully designed to save our lives from short-term immediate dangers—was destroying me from the inside out. As the hours stretched into days, and days into weeks, and weeks into months, I was experiencing the good, the bad, and the ugly sides of stress.

A FRESH PARADIGM

In 1966, Clint Eastwood starred in an iconic Western about three characters: *The Good, the Bad and the Ugly.* There were some nice twists in the plot, but the audience knew that, in the end, the Good would prevail over the Bad and the Ugly.

We can categorize stress responses the same way. Some are good ones; some are bad ones; and—as Dick experienced after losing his job—other stressors can get downright ugly. Unfortunately, life doesn't always work out like the movies. No script ensures good is going to triumph over bad in the end. How would Dick's movie end? How will *your* movie end? From our perspective, it's up to each of us to write our own script on how our own movies might end. And this is the most amazing thing about stress—it drives us toward change, but how we change is up to us. The stressor does not determine that; rather how we respond will determine the outcome. In other words, how we respond to stress will determine if our future will be good, bad, or ugly.

To get started, let's create a fresh paradigm that identifies and analyzes the good, bad, and ugly character traits of stressors. The paradigm includes three opposing couplets:

⊙ Eustress and Distress

⊙ Physical and Mental

⊙ Chronic and Acute

Let's unpack the meaning of each of these traits.

The Good: Eustress

Eu-stress /**yoo**'stres *noun*: a positive form of stress having a beneficial effect on health, motivation, performance, and emotional well-being.[12]

"Eu" is a Greek prefix that stands for "good." So eustress is good stress.

Eustress:

⊙ Motivates

⊙ Feels energizing

⊙ Is perceived to be within your abilities

⊙ Feels exciting

⊙ Improves performance

The Bad: Distress

Dis-tress/ de'-**stres** *noun*: extreme anxiety, sorrow, or pain.

Synonyms for *distress* include suffering, anguish, agony, pain, heartache, torment, heartbreak, wretchedness, misery, grief, sorrow, woe, desolation, and despair.

When distress shows up on the scene, it

- ⊙ Causes anxiety or concern

- ⊙ Can be short term or long term

- ⊙ May be perceived as outside our coping abilities

- ⊙ Feels unpleasant

- ⊙ Decreases performance

- ⊙ Can lead to mental and physiological damage[13]

The Paralyzing Impact of Fear

Do you find yourself worrying too much or being afraid of what could happen to you? Sometimes a little worry is warranted, but often it paralyzes us from achieving our goals or getting done what we are perfectly capable of doing. Some people can't seem to stop worrying. Indeed, about 15 percent of the population can be found in this category. What we now know is that worry itself is not the problem; rather it is the ability of worry to distract and prevent you from accomplishing those goals that are important to you. To help you identify and face your fears, take the time to answer these questions:

1.   What worries you most of the time?

2.   How is this worry affecting you?

3.   What have you done to try to reduce this worry?

4.   What is the worst possible outcome, and how likely is it to actually happen?

5.   What is most likely to happen, and what options do you have to deal with that outcome should it occur?

Set aside a time and place to worry, and then when you are done, get up and do something else. Your worry session is over. If the concerns come up again, simply tell yourself you will worry about them later at your next worry session. You see, worry per se is not all bad. Only when worry and anxiety overtake your day can they become disabling. In addition, many of the stress-reduction activities in this book work equally well in lowering your fears and anxieties.

Physical and Mental Stressors

Physical stressors place physiological tension and/or pressure on your *body*. Mental stressors cause psychological tension and/or pressure on your *thinking*. In reality, it's hard to tell where the body ends and thinking begins (as we will discuss later).

The Physical

Stressors come in many different forms and categories. Think of physical stressors as occurrences that place mechanical pressure or tension on your body, such as:

⊙ Running

⊙ Infection

⊙ Jumping

⊙ Breathing

⊙ Digesting

Most of the time, your body will naturally adjust to physical stressors and you won't even be aware of it. For example, if you generate too much of a particular chemical, enzymes are there to break it down. If you push your body too hard through extreme exercise, your body will eventually shut down to give you some rest whether you want it or not. Eventually, bones and muscles will heal, and your immune system will vanquish the infection.

The Mental

Mental stressors come from thoughts. If you are thinking about something and worried about its outcome—whether it's a test, a personal problem, or a project at work—simply thinking about it places pressure and tension on the brain.

Mental stressors can trigger stress responses even when nothing is truly happening. The stressor happens in your brain, *and yet your body reacts as if it's a real physical threat* (more explanation on this later). Are you concerned about the future? Trying to figure out a complicated relational issue? Did you just get a letter from a collection agency? All these mental stressors can cause complex emotional responses. These emotional components are hard to get ahold of because they are buried in the complexities of the brain.

⊙   It's the fear when you can't predict what will
    happen.

⊙   It's the sadness when you can't fix something that
    is broken.

⊙   It's the anger when your goals and desires are
    being blocked and denied.

Mental stressors are often precipitated by a long-term sense of injustice or the loss of something (such as Dick getting fired), or they might come from a short-term predicament (such as Nick's thumb being stuck in an alligator's mouth). Keep in mind that the distinction between physical and mental stressors is somewhat artificial. That's because they often occur together. For example, through pain and discomfort, physical stressors may well trigger emotional responses, which can independently trigger physical responses.

In the short term, psychological stressors aid your survival and growth. They force you to come up with solutions that are better, like how to get your thumb out of a gator's mouth. Short-term mental stressors are usually "the Good." Long-term mental stressors are often "the Bad."

Long-Term and Short-Term Stressors

The technical word for long term is "chronic," and for short term it is "acute."

The story is told about two friends who were being chased by a bear through the woods. One of them stopped to tie his running shoes. His friend just laughed. "There's no way you're going to outrun that bear."

"I know," the other friend replied. "I only have to outrun *you*."

If a bear is chasing you, your brain and body do everything they can to give you a chance to survive. Most the time you think and act faster when the stress response kicks in. Stressors rev us up quickly to address an immediate threat.

- ⊙ Something goes "bump" in the night.

- ⊙ You get hit in the face with a snowball.

- ⊙ Your ex-boyfriend texts.

- ⊙ You hear the blast of a siren behind you.

But let's revisit the faster-running friend who didn't become bear food. What happens in his body and brain when he experiences ongoing guilt and remorse for abandoning his buddy? What if he becomes constantly paranoid that a bear is always waiting to attack? That's when the stressor becomes a long-term or chronic pressure.

- ⊙ You constantly fear someone will break into your house.

- ⊙ Your current boyfriend is verbally abusive.

- ⊙ You live downtown where sirens are constantly blaring.

- ⊙ A relative you barely know unexpectedly comes to live with you.

Remember, triggers turn on the stress response. Repeated and continual stressors can not only trigger the stress response but *keep* it on. Consider the repetition of an angry thought, the constantly triggered memory of a painful experience, a chronic lack of sleep, the continuous agony of an important loss. These long-term mental stressors cause long-term problems when the stress response doesn't turn off as it should or when you can't predict when it will end. The days of the coronavirus pandemic are a prime example of how these factors can, in many people, be as disruptive to their health and well-being as the symptoms of the disease. The social isolation experienced during the peak of the 2020 pandemic caused negative consequences, both emotionally and physically, over time.

The Matrix

To review, stressors can be characterized along three different paradigms:

- ⊙ Eustress and Distress

- ⊙ Physical and Mental

- ⊙ Long Term and Short Term

When you put them all together, this gives you eight different combinations of stressors to consider.

- ⊙ Short-term mental eustress: Hearing a good joke. Figuring out a Sudoku. Studying for a test.

- ⊙ Short-term mental distress: Seeing an "F" on a test, then realizing it belongs to someone else. Getting an email from your oncologist, then seeing your results were benign.

- ⊙ Short-term physical eustress: A massage. Taking long, deep breaths.

- ⊙ Short-term physical distress: Getting a flu shot. Stubbing your toe.

- ⊙ Long-term mental eustress: Taking a relaxing vacation. Reading a favorite novel. Praying regularly.

- ⊙ Long-term mental distress: Financial struggles. Unresolved conflict with a former spouse. Unruly teenagers.

- ⊙ Long-term physical eustress: Regular moderate exercise. Healthy diet.

- ⊙ Long-term physical distress: Chronic lack of sleep. A diet high in fats and sugars.

Eustressors and Distressors Are Relative

The same stressors affect different people in very different ways. Nick thrives on long-distance endurance sports. He recently rode his bicycle more than three thousand miles from Seattle, Washington, to Tampa, Florida, to raise money for charity. He lives for this sort of adventure. It's eustress to him, whereas the mere thought of doing something like that causes significant distress in others. But Nick is a professor, too, and if he gets a message from his dean saying, "Why didn't you submit your grades on time?" *then* Nick goes into panic mode. Dick, on the other hand, is a gifted administrator; keeping track of details like deadlines comes easily for him. But the thought of having to ride a bike thousands of miles? That would be a major stressor (unless the bike had a motor in it like his Harley. That would be pure eustress for him!). These are examples of an important point: The same stressors will trigger different people differently in different situations.

Physical and Mental Stressors Are Inseparable

In the 1920s and 1930s, scientists had long debates about the relationship between emotions and stress responses. Do emotions originate in the brain? Or do they originate in the body? Do you run away because you are afraid? Or are you afraid because you're running away? The answer—as is so often the case when studying humans—is "yes." The emotion drives the physiology, *and* the physiology drives the emotion. If your physical senses don't experience something as a threat, nothing is going to happen because the physiology feeds the brain's perception.

Furthermore, we now understand that thoughts and memories are entities that depend upon the DNA, proteins, and neurological networks of the physical brain. Many of the estimated eighty-six billion neurons in the brain are directly or indirectly connected to the entire body through the brain stem and spinal cord. It's impossible to tell where one starts and the other ends. That's why a professional chess player, in the midst of a tournament, can have the same elevated blood pressures and heart rate as a runner in the midst of a marathon. This was dramatically illustrated with Grandmaster chess players. Heart rates during a chess match could easily rise to 170 to 180 BPM. Keep in mind that little to no physical activity takes place during a chess match; this rise in heart rate was caused solely by mental stressors and the pressure to perform—not to make mistakes—to win.[14]

For the chess player, the stressor is purely mental. For the marathon runner, it's physical. But they both experience similar physiological responses.

Physical, mental, and emotional stressors often merge in relationships. Social interaction is critical from childhood all the way to adulthood. Children who are deprived of physical contact with their mother are stunted both physiologically and psychologically. This in turn affects growth-promoting chemicals produced by the body. And this trend does not stop with infants. Once the growth period is over for humans, the growth factors mostly work at rebuilding and remodeling.

The Ugly: Long-Term Mental Distress

The "perfect storm" takes place when long-term mental triggers keep the stress response ignited. Truly life-threatening events are relatively uncommon in the modern world. What we do have is an unnatural number of mental stressors that the body is not designed to endure. This was exemplified by the arrival of a new strain of highly contagious coronavirus, which rapidly evolved into a worldwide pandemic in 2020. The virus's impact upon personal health was magnified for many by anxiety stemming from the sudden loss of income, bleak statistics, and uncertainty about when the panic would end. Lack of control, inability to predict, and, during the early stages, little if any reason to be optimistic made for a perfect storm. How ironic that at the very moment people needed a robust immune system, it was threatened by stress-related emotions. That was on top of the everyday stressors mentioned previously.

Long-term mental distress can come from a single stressor that's repeatedly interpreted as negative and significant—as in Dick losing his job. It can also come from many small stressors that add up to the equivalent effect of a major ongoing catastrophe. In the modern world, long-term stress is often triggered by an endless stream of short-term aggravations that happen on a daily basis, none of which would be significant by themselves. Get the kids off to school + rush-hour traffic + your secretary didn't get the report you needed + short lunch break + thinking about the sales meeting in the afternoon + trying to get all e-mails out before five o'clock + the PTA meeting that goes long into the evening. They all add up and equal long-term mental distress.

What are the effects? Things can get pretty ugly, can't they?

Think about it this way: The stress response is designed to save your life from an *immediate* physical threat. This is often referred to as the *fight-or-flight* reaction when we encounter circumstances that make us feel fearful. The stress response directs maximum resources toward the organ systems that will give the best chance of surviving. But these resources must come from somewhere, so the stress response minimizes the resources going to other organ systems in the body that are not absolutely essential for surviving the *immediate* crisis—even though those systems are important for medium- and long-term health.

The main systems that can shut down when the body needs to conserve energy for the primary task of survival include the following.

Immunity

Your immune system is designed to protect you from disease-causing microbial organisms. But when the brain perceives an immediate threat, the stress response diverts energy to the systems that are necessary for immediate survival, sometimes at the expense of your ability to fight disease. (Under some conditions, stress can mobilize your immune system. But that's another story, which we'll omit for now as we stick with what happens most of the time.) It's a great strategy until the trigger switch gets left on by your brain when no real physical threat exists. In this situation, certain stress-related hormones can impair your immune system. Who cares if you might get influenza next winter if you don't survive and make it through the fall? Long-term stressors can decrease your defenses against illness and infection. No wonder many people become ill more often when under long-term stress. Dick experienced this every year when he took his vacation. After a long winter and spring of working, he would work extra hard the two weeks prior to his vacation in order to not only catch up but to get ahead. Then by day three of his vacation, he would inevitably get sick. All that stress affected his immunity, which meant when something was in the air, he caught it. Sustained, long-term stress can exacerbate many diseases including cardiovascular disease, gastric ulcers, fibromyalgia, and autoimmune diseases such as lupus and rheumatoid arthritis.

In fact, bad relationships can worsen your health. For example, while the presence of a spouse generally benefits immune function, a marriage wrought with conflict and turmoil can have the opposite effect. Studies show that when quality of marriage is a variable, people in poorer-quality relationships are more stressed and depressed than those in better-quality relationships. And as we have learned, both stress and depression dysregulate immune function.[15] Indeed, compared to more happily married people, people in distressed relationships had smaller antibody responses to an influenza virus vaccine.[16] Furthermore, individuals in more distressed marriages had evidence of greater Epstein-Barr virus (EBV) activation compared with those in less distressed marriages.[17] Negative and hostile behaviors expressed during a conflict—such as blaming or interrupting the other person—appear to be particularly detrimental, as reflected in elevated inflammation. So taking the time to nurture your relationships has real value. You will be better off for the effort in so many ways.

Digestion

Digesting food during a life-threatening, short-term stress event is the equivalent of going to the hardware store to buy building supplies for a remodel during a hurricane. Think about it: If a hurricane is bearing down on your house, you wouldn't be remodeling your kitchen. You'd be in crisis mode and diverting your energy to the most immediate vulnerabilities. That's basically what the body does. It shuts down your digestion and starts burning energy from stored sources. That's an excellent strategy for short-term survival, but in the long term, it leads to ulcers, acid reflux, and a serious depletion of energy reserves.

Memory

Who cares what's in your long-term memory if you're not going to be around to remember it? Your body doesn't. That's why during a short-term crisis your brain focuses mental attention on immediate survival. But that's also why people who are under chronic stress become forgetful in the moment and have long-term memory problems later. This problem was first observed in the survivors of Nazi concentration camps.

Remember the basics: The human stress responses are designed to save your life from short-term acute threats. But when the trigger switch is left on and the stress response is continually triggered through long-term mental and physical stressors, you're going to have problems down the road.

Symptoms of Long-Term Mental and/or Physical Distress

PHYSICAL SYMPTOMS		
Tension headaches	Night sweats	Difficulty reaching orgasm
Heartburn	Increased sensitivity to light and/or sound	Problem swallowing
Frowning	Cold, sweaty hands	Frequent colds or bouts with flu
Stomach cramps	Cold hands and feet	Appetite change
Trembling of lips or hands	Lightheadedness	Fatigue
Nausea	Flatulence or belching	Hives
Difficulty breathing	Faintness or dizziness	Insomnia or hypersomnia
Muscle tension	Frequent urination	Rashes
Restlessness	Ringing in the ears	Weight change
Neck aches	Constipation	Chills or goose bumps
Back pain	Enlarged pupils	Digestive upset
Heart and chest pain	Nervous diarrhea	Pounding heart
Aggressive body language	Blushing	Rapid heartbeat
Increased perspiration	Decreased sexual desire	Shortness of breath
Jaw pain	Dry mouth	Autoimmune symptoms

MENTAL SYMPTOMS

Anxiety	Depression	Suspiciousness
Suicidal thoughts	Poor concentration	Confusion
Guilt	Nightmares	Whirling mind
Fear of closeness to people	Low productivity	Indecision
Increased anger	Trouble learning	No new ideas
Frustration	Negative attitude	Feeling overwhelmed
Loneliness	Forgetfulness	Boredom
Moodiness	Defensiveness	Discontentment
Dulled senses	Disorganization	Spacing out

BEHAVIORAL SYMPTOMS

Inattention to grooming	Lying	Overreaction
Perfectionism	Increased alcohol use	Mood swings
Increased tardiness	Making excuses	Prone to minor accidents
Reduced productivity	Increased tobacco use	Bad temper
Serious appearance	Social withdrawal	Crying spells
Fast or mumbled speech	Gambling	Easily discouraged
Unusual behavior	Self-pity	Stuttering
Unusual risk taking	Overspending	Procrastination
Nervous habits	Strained communication	Nervous laughing
Gritting of teeth	Edginess	Nail-biting
Rushing around or pacing	Frustration	Excessive worrying

If you've been under long-term chronic stressors, important systems are being compromised. This stress will eventually catch up with you and take a serious toll on your entire body. It's like a high-interest-rate credit card that you've maxed out for immediate needs. You need to get some money back in the bank for the long haul. You can't just keep taking it out.

We suggest these three steps to turn around long-term stressors:

1. Find ways to change your perceptions.

2. Address those triggers that normally activate that response.

3. Practice ways to get the response under control.

We will unpack all of this in easy-to-understand ways. In the end, you will have all the tools and a practical strategy for minimizing the bad and the ugly while embracing all that is good about stressors.

The Science Behind It: Psychosomatic and More

Psychosomatic is a compound word made from two Greek words: *psyche* ("mind") and *somatikos* ("body"). Scientists debate about the meaning of the word *psychosomatic*, but it's generally understood to relate to the interconnected relationships between the mental and the physical. This was a big revelation when their interconnectedness was first being discovered. Now there is little doubt. Can your thoughts really affect your body and vice versa? Of course.

Psychogenic fever, for example, is a stress-related psychosomatic disease. Some patients (usually young women) develop extremely high core body temperatures (up to 41°C/105°F) during acute emotional events and develop fevers (around 38°C/100°F) during long-term mental stress.

The psychosomatic connection is now well established between long-term mental stressors and memory, the immune system, and many ailments such as coronary heart disease and diabetes. How does this work on a biomedical level?

- ⊙ First, a sensory signal arrives in the amygdala, a part of the brain responsible in part for initiating responses to anger and fear.

- ⊙ At the same time, the hippocampus processes memories and thoughts to be stored in the cortex. This stored information about previous outcomes of similar situations is compared to the incoming sensory information.

- ⊙ If the situation is interpreted as dangerous, a warning message is sent to the hypothalamus, triggering the sympathetic nervous system and the stress responses, which releases hormones like cortisol.

⊙ Cortisol and norepinephrine create additional energy and turn on some organs in your body while shutting others off. Perhaps the first organ to respond is your heart. It immediately starts beating faster. This is why heart rate is used as a proxy for stress. The higher the heart rate, the greater your stress. Conversely, the lower your heart rate, the lower your stress.

⊙ When the brain receives signals telling you the crisis is over, the fight-or-flight response is turned off, bringing down the heart rate, respiration rate, and cortisol to normal levels.

But—and this is the important part—if thoughts and memories keep telling the hypothalamus that a threat is present, the whole system stays on high alert, continually injecting cortisol into the body. That's when the destruction starts to take place. The long-term release of cortisol, triggered by the chronic stress, damages the hippocampus. And since the hippocampus regulates the processing of memory, long-term memory can be diminished.

The long-term release of cortisol also affects your body's capacity to fight off disease and illness. The conductor of the immune system is a type of white blood cell that coordinates the activity of most of the others. It responds to cortisol in one of two ways: a small amount can stimulate it, while large amounts have the potential to inhibit it. Thus, cortisol is largely responsible for keeping your immune system in an optimal state. Problems arise when a stressor continues for weeks or even months with no end in sight. That's when the normal controls can sometimes be short-circuited as the immune system is pushed by cortisol and other chemicals below the threshold where it can fight infection.

DICK TIBBITS: NOT EVEN A PINK SLIP, PART 2

Hindsight is always 20-20. I look back now and wish I had known at the time of my "reengineering" what I know now. I was stuck in the vicious cycle of long-term mental distress.

The turning point came the day a close friend decided to simply listen to me. He had tried to tell me what to do in the past, but I wasn't ready to listen. So he came just to be with me, to listen. He shared my pain as best he could. He had questions— questions I wasn't willing to ask myself. But he asked without trying to solve anything. He didn't argue. He didn't judge. He just kept probing and listening, probing and listening. He also shared his own pain from watching me, his capable friend, crumble before his eyes.

"Tell me what you really *think."*

"What did it feel like when... ?"

He sat with me for the longest time, often just being present and attentive; slowly I was able to put words to thoughts I didn't even know I was thinking. By the time he left, I had begun to think outside the mental box that had imprisoned me for far too long.

A thin ray of light began to shine into the darkness.

Hope.

Not much, but enough. Enough hope to take a new job.

I finally took a position at AdventHealth Celebration—a joint venture between Disney and AdventHealth. What an opportunity—an opportunity that would have never come my way if I were still working at my previous job. And I would have never met Nick.

It was a huge pay cut, and I was down the totem pole compared to the position I previously held. It was an awkward start that turned into a wonderful ending. I had a routine again and a reason to get out of bed in the morning. My efforts and skills were recognized, a much-needed affirmation of my self-worth. And the job gave my life purpose and meaning. What I was doing was not only helping me; more importantly, I was helping others again. My thoughts were positive. I was active, eating better, and engaged with others on a daily basis. I was back in life and no longer sitting on the sidelines.

Five years after I had been fired, the circumstances all came full circle when I was offered the position of vice president of human resources—a significant promotion and a double-edged sword. I would be responsible for communicating to employees both when they were doing their jobs well and when they were not doing their jobs well.

I started thinking about every employee I would have to

meet—especially those I would have to tell would be losing their job for one reason or another. I knew the shock they would feel and the financial stress they would experience. I knew they would have to go home and tell their spouse and kids. From the depths of my heart, all the agony and tears came back. But over the years my experiences made me better able to communicate genuine concern and understanding for what they would go through. Together, God and I had rewritten the script of my "movie." In this new position I could offer words to help others rewrite their scripts as well.

"I know this is difficult."

"You will be going through some things. I've been through them."

"You're not just disappearing."

"Don't hesitate to call me if you have questions or anything you want to comment on. You can call me tomorrow or next week."

Is it possible I went through excruciating pain and long-term mental distress for a greater purpose? I couldn't see it at the time, but I do now. I took the Ugly that had come from the Bad and caused it all to work together for Good by making me a more gentle, wise, and compassionate leader. I had become a wounded healer, one who, because of his own wounds, could better understand and be a healing force for the wounds of others.

THE MOST IMPORTANT STRESS IN YOUR WORLD

We've covered a lot of ground in this chapter. We can boil it all down to the summary that stressors can be good, bad, or downright ugly. We looked at important theories and scientific explanations for how some of this works.

So what about you personally? Yes, you are experiencing all kinds of stressors right now. But could we venture to say that your most *important* stress right now, in this moment, is still the one that motivated you to pick up this book? You feel it. You know it. A tension and a pressure exist between what is and what you desire, between your reality and your vision.

You are in the best position to accurately reflect upon your feelings. *Think. Listen. Pray.* And when you grasp this inner tension, you'll realize this is not only the most *important* stressor, but it can also become the *best* kind of stressor possible. For it is not the stressor that determines the good, bad, or ugly; rather how you respond to that stressor will make all the difference in the world for you.

You have one shot at this life, and you know it. As Alexander Hamilton says in the popular Broadway play, "I'm not throwing away my shot!" You have one shot to chase hidden dreams, to heal unknown wounds, to find inner peace and balance, and to realize the lingering hope for true, transforming life change.

Hold on to those thoughts as we head into the next chapter, and we will unpack them in the context of an innovative new paradigm.

RELEASE YOUR TENSION ONE MUSCLE AT A TIME

Part 2 is coming. Just one more chapter before we jump headfirst into the pool full of the best short-term and long-term Stress Recovery Strategies ever discovered. We hope you're already trying out the deep breathing exercise from the last chapter and realizing, "Yes, I think this works!" So let's add to your deep breathing a simple "tense-and-release" exercise called progressive muscle relaxation. Here is what to do:

From either a standing or sitting position, let your arms relax at your side with all your fingers gently pulled by gravity toward the floor.

- ⊙ Lie on your back on the floor.

- ⊙ Starting with your feet, tense up your toes and arches for three to five seconds and then release the tension.

- ⊙ Let your feet become totally relaxed.

- ⊙ Take three slow, deep breaths, further relaxing on each exhale.

- ⊙ Repeat this routine two to three times.

- ⊙ Do the same with each major muscle group, moving up your body: your calves, your stomach, your chest and shoulders, your arms and hands, and finally your head with special emphasis on the temple area.

⊙ After completing each muscle group, lie motionless for five minutes, focusing on your breath and relaxing deeply on each exhale.

⊙ Take your time getting up so you don't get dizzy.

Simple, isn't it? It's easy, short-term eustress for your body and brain. Go ahead. Try it.

CHAPTER 2 TAKEAWAYS

A Fresh Paradigm

Stressors can be good, bad, and ugly. The stressors that trigger our stress responses can be broken down along three continuums.

⊙ Eustress and Distress

⊙ Physical and Mental

⊙ Chronic and Acute

The Good: Eustress

Eustress is a positive form of stress having a beneficial effect on health, motivation, performance, and emotional well-being.

The Bad: Distress

Distress is associated with anxiety, sorrow, or pain and includes suffering, anguish, agony, heartache, torment, heartbreak, wretchedness, misery, grief, sorrow, woe, desolation, and despair.

Physical Stressors

Physical stressors place physical tension and/or pressure on the *body*.

Mental Stressors

Mental stressors cause psychological tension and/or pressure that come from your thoughts.

Long-Term and Short-Term Stressors

The technical name for long-term is *chronic*; the technical name for short-term is *acute*. The stress response is designed to deal with immediate acute threats to your physical well-being. Long-term mental stressors cause long-term problems when the stress response doesn't turn off as it should.

Because of the incredible complexity of the body and neurological systems, nothing is black and white. The difference between "eustressors" and "distressors" is highly dependent on the person and the situation. Physical and mental stressors are so intertwined that you have to consider them to be one.

The Ugly: Long-Term Mental Distress

When the stress response system remains in the "on" position for an extended period of time—as it often does in the modern world—your immune system, digestion, memory, and reproductive capabilities can be significantly impacted.

The Science Behind It: Psychosomatic and More

The brain is an astounding biological wonder that is inseparably linked with everything that happens in our bodies. Different regions of the brain work together with a cocktail of neurotransmitters and hormones. Long-term mental stress, however, throws everything out of balance with destructive results. The right tools and a simple strategy will allow you to minimize the bad and the ugly while embracing all that is good.

The Most Important Stress in Your World

The most important pressure and stress in your life is the gap that exists between reality and what you hope for. The best way to deal with this is to take the first steps to realizing your dreams. They don't have to be fulfilled today, but you do need to see progress and a light at the end of the tunnel.

CHAPTER 3

THE OPTIMAL ZONE

Goldilocks Knew Her Stuff

NICK HALL: THE H$_2$O ZONE, PART 1

*W*hat he started was, at the time, pushing a lot of boundaries. He figured it would be easier to ask forgiveness than to get permission—or, better yet, maybe we could pass through in stealth mode undetected. My friend Steve Isaac came up with the idea. It was one of those ideas that some people think should have leaked through a hole at the bottom of his bucket list and never been pursued. But the rest of us thought it was a terrific idea: race three hundred miles from St. Petersburg, Florida, through the Everglades to Key Largo. On alternate years, make that a twelve-hundred-mile circumnavigation of Florida. On the water. In human/wind-powered boats. Passing through the initially forbidden waters of the Everglades. The idea stuck, and in 2001 the Everglades Challenge was born.*

We took on code names and communicated via radio with aliases such as "Dirty Little Runner Gal," "Paddle Carver," "Tyro," and "Shark Chow." Steve, our leader, was "Chief." I picked the alias "Pelican" because I thought it fit. They're not as attractive, fast, or agile as other birds, but they get the job done. Collectively, we are known as the Water Tribe, a ragtag bunch facing the elements in canoes, kayaks, and small sailing vessels, all competing to finish and claim the grand prize: a shark tooth you could buy at Walmart for about three dollars.

I've competed in these events since 2002, all of them epic adventures in their own right. But in 2019? That year was in a league all its own. That's when instead of paddling solo, I captained a team of three kayaks along with my son-in-law Joey, a highly athletic and capable firefighter, and Julie, a fellow Water Triber and accomplished sailor. I wasn't worried about them. They were each over eighteen and had signed the ominous event release form promising all sorts of pain and excruciating forms of death if not fully prepared. But I was worried about the most precious co-captains in the form of my thirteen-year-old grandson Jackson, his twelve-year-old cousin James, and his sister Abigail, who had just turned eleven.

It's maybe not quite as crazy as you think. We were attempting the shorter Everglades Challenge, covering a mere three hundred miles from St. Petersburg to Key Largo. We trained hard and planned hard. I had run the team through a two-day "dress rehearsal" in heavy winds and large waves. Even when Julie had an incapacitating allergic reaction, the team rose to the occasion and showed great adaptability in the face of unforeseen stressors. I was confident in them. We had exceptionally seaworthy Hobie Tandem Island kayaks. Unlike most kayaks, they can be powered by sail, paddle, or pedals. (I need to use the pedals a lot because of permanent arthritis in my right thumb, courtesy of the alligator I jumped on when a teenager.) I incessantly checked our supply lists. I knew the route well. When we pushed our tiny, sail-driven boats into the surf, I felt in control. I had a good prediction of what lay ahead, and, yes, I had it all planned out.

But there is a military axiom that says, "No plan survives first contact with the enemy."

(To be continued)

Front row: Nick's grandchildren James, Abigail, and Jackson
Back row: Nick's son-in-law Joey, fellow Water Triber Julie, and Nick

Abbey helping Jackson and James launch their kayak for the Everglades Challenge

INTO THE ZONE

Life is a lot like the Everglades Challenge. We launch each day with a plan and expectations. We have hopes, dreams, visions, and strategies that are soon challenged by stressors we can neither control nor predict. The key to surviving and thriving is to be prepared, to thoughtfully manage those stressors, and to keep them in an optimal range in intense circumstances. Everyone, along their life journey, faces the same issues; like the Everglades Challenge, life itself truly is a matter of life and death.

To assist you on your journey, we offer three simple concepts that will get you started on your journey against distress.

- ⊙ Some stressors you can control and predict.

- ⊙ Some stressors you cannot control or predict.

⊙   Any given stressor has an optimal range of
      intensity, in any given person, in any given
      situation, at any given time.

These truths will lead us into power principles that can
redefine your journey through life.

Most people tend to view stress as bad. But if we think
in terms of eustress and distress, everything looks different.
And it should. Whether it's physical or mental, an ideal level
of tension or pressure brings out the best in us. We call it the
Optimal Zone. This concept was developed in 1908 in Boston
by Drs. Yerkes and Dodson.[18]

The illustration of stress along the continuum of a bell
curve helps visualize the effects of too little stress, too much
stress, and the optimal level of stress, the Optimal Zone.

The Stress Bell Curve

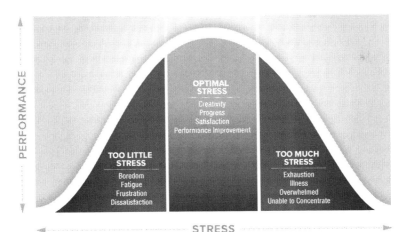

When you are in the Optimal Zone, you are in:

- ⊙ A place of balance

- ⊙ A place of power

- ⊙ A place of efficiency

- ⊙ A place of purpose

- ⊙ A place of confidence

- ⊙ A place of tranquility

Everyone wants to have more energy, a more robust immune system, and to get their life on track. Consequently, we will all benefit from techniques that put us in our own personal Optimal Zones. Think *Goldilocks and the Three Bears.*

- ⊙ Food too hot? You are going to get burned.

- ⊙ Food too cold? It's going to be bland and boring.

- ⊙ Bed too hard? It's going to be difficult to rest.

- ⊙ Bed too soft? Call your chiropractor in the morning.

Goldilocks had it right: You want balance. You want to be in the middle of the extremes; you want it to be just right.

TOO HOT

We've been conditioned to view excessive stressors and unhealthy stress responses as an unavoidable reality. Our culture even affirms being "all stressed out" as a virtue—as if it's part of our personal and national identity. But the bottom line is that excessive stressors cause distress. If circumstances are being pushed toward the right side of the curve, the likelihood increases that you'll make a careless mistake, do something you'll later regret, break something, or the like.

If your stressors are not managed properly, or if you don't increase your capacity to respond to them, you will reach a point where your performance drops—and it may drop significantly. Heart rate and blood pressure are a big part of this process, and they are two of the most reliable indicators that conditions are starting to be pushed to your extreme. Whether physical or mental, excessive stressors that you endure for the long term put you on the road headed for trouble.

With athletes, we use heart rate as a way of monitoring stress. When a heart rate is too high, judgment is impaired, mistakes happen, and performance suffers. When a heart rate is too low, the athlete is just following the crowd and thus not performing at their best. You may want to start wearing a heart rate monitor and track the variations in your heart rate throughout the day. In a future chapter we will discuss how you can determine your personal Optimal Zone and what to do when you are not there.

TOO COLD

On the left side of the curve, we have the opposite problem. Too few stressors in any given situation decrease performance as well. For example, students often need to take tests to provide the motivation to study.

Athletes (and everyone else with a heartbeat) need physical movement and exercise. Spiritually, we need stressors to keep us motivated in our pursuit of purpose, meaning, and God. Yet many of us have resigned ourselves to sedentary lives that make us lethargic, passive, and stagnant in one or many areas.

The naïve view that all stress should be reduced as much as possible is unrealistic and detrimental to your health. Too little stress diminishes your ability to perform well in your job. Research shows that people who have routine jobs that don't challenge them have more stress than those whose work challenges them.[19] They are also more dissatisfied with their jobs, which adds to the stress of going to work every day at the same place doing the same task. This process can create a downward chain reaction for all involved.

The "eat, sleep, eat, sleep" stress management technique might be helpful for some people some of the time, but not for all, and not all the time.

If you think that all stressors are bad, all you can do is lower your expectations or change your perceptions of reality. In some situations, that's a great idea, but it is not the final solution. If you lower your expectations too far, you'll be bored. If you succeed in reducing your stressors to zero, you'll be, well, dead.

JUST RIGHT!

There *is* an optimal range of intensity of any given stressor, for any given person, in any given situation, at any given time. Physically, mentally, and spiritually, the quest is to find life balance near the center of the Optimal Zone. From there, the ideal is to continually monitor and make adjustments to keep this dynamic balance intact. When that happens, you have a sense of "I've got this!" Everything seems to be in harmony and functioning at maximum potential. But this doesn't simply happen. Every individual has to find ways to achieve this balance.

Simple enough. But then, of course, the process starts to get complicated, because this "optimal range" varies in any given person, in any given situation, at any given time. Because of our individual complexities, one size never fits all. Many variables can impact your ability to cope with whatever life throws at you. These variables include:

Relationships

The number of friends a person has—especially the number of close friends—is a huge factor in modulating the stress response. A study carried out at the Common Cold Unit in England examined the impact of friends upon the incidence of catching a cold. Participants volunteered to have the cold virus infused into their nasal passages. Those who had the most long-term, deep friendships were less likely to catch a cold compared with those with few friends. In addition, if those with more friends did get sick, they experienced fewer days suffering from cold symptoms.[20] Studies in wild chimpanzees indicate this effect is likely due to the ability of social support to reduce the release of stress hormones that comprise the brain-pituitary-adrenal axis.[21]

Friendship

Friends make a real difference in your mental and physical well-being. But making new friends can be difficult. Making friends can both stress you and benefit you. *Will they like me? What do I talk about? How do I start a conversation when everyone is talking with someone else?* These and other questions can leave us sitting on the sidelines in the midst of a crowd. Conversations can be impossible to start or difficult to keep going, leaving you anxious and wanting to exit as quickly as possible and go home. If this sounds like you, we have good news for you. You are not alone. Many people have a difficult time making friends. Some have even given up trying. Approximately sixty million people in the United States (about 20 percent of the population)[22] report feeling lonely. But there is hope. New research is providing answers for why people are lonely and what to do about it.

Here are a few practical tips for getting started in making new friends.

1. Go out to where people are. Don't sit home alone because you are fearful. This will only make things worse for you.

2. Go to something where you share a common interest with others who are attending. This gives you something immediately to talk about.

3. Ask people about themselves; then listen. People like to talk about what they are doing, and this will help you break the ice.

4. Recognize that in initial meetings, you don't want to monopolize someone's time. They are not your best friend; they are someone you just met. Give time for relationships to develop. And remember that not everyone will turn out to be a good friend. So don't put all your eggs into one basket; keep reaching out.

5. With practice and persistence, you will start to build your list of friends.

Personal History

Your history, and in particular your childhood experiences, can directly affect how you handle stress. For example, how much adversity have you had in your life and how intense were those experiences from your past? Your life experiences will help determine whether stress paralyzes you or motivates you. Excessive punishments during your upbringing may prompt you to give in too quickly in order to bring an end to the conflict. On the other hand, if you're used to getting your way, you may respond to resistance by throwing an adult temper tantrum in the hope that you can intimidate the other person to back off. If you have too much adversity in your past history, you may tend to overreact by either giving in too quickly or by becoming aggressive too quickly. Either approach may or may not be helpful in your current situation. So rather than reacting the way you have in the past, consider how you want to respond in the present, and chart a new history for yourself going forward.

Gender

Men and women tend to respond to stressors differently. The rule in the biological and behavioral sciences is exceptions will always exist, and that certainly applies here. Because of the influence of certain body chemicals during early development, a woman's brain is more likely to develop in ways that cause her to value relationships more than achievement. On the other hand, exposure to different chemicals steers a man's brain to place a higher value on achievement.[23] These biases are clearly influenced by cultural variables as well. In general, the primary trigger of the stress responses in women is more likely to be centered around a troubled relationship. But men are more likely to unravel at the emotional seams following the loss of a job or anything that interferes with the achievement of an objective.

Coping Ability

How much control a person has will impact their ability to cope with adversity. The more control you *perceive* you have, the more you'll be able to manage stressors.[24] Your ability to predict what is likely to occur next increases your capacity to handle stressors as well.[25]

Attitude

And your level of optimism? You guessed it. Believing that circumstances will eventually improve increases your capacity to handle distressful circumstances better.[26, 27]

Social Type

How you relate to others has a significant effect on how you deal with stressors. Some people are loners because of personality (introverts, for example). Some people are loners because of desire. (Think of the person who says, "I can get more done on my own with less interference.") There is a clear distinction between feeling lonely and being socially isolated, between loneliness (the lack of meaningful relationships in one's life) and solitude (the desired separation from people). The difference in the experience, however, is often determined by an individual's uniquenesses.[28]

Age

The older we get, the longer it takes to recover from distress. Indeed, a prominent neuroscientist, Robert Sapolsky of Stanford University, has suggested taking longer to recover from stress might be a valid definition of aging.[29]

The list goes on and on. Exercise and diet are prominent factors, as are medical conditions and medications. Other factors include genetics, early life experiences, and epigenetic factors. Some people thrive on uncertainty and enjoy risk. Others strive for stability and security. A person's threshold for emotional excitement is most likely coded in their genetic blueprint.

That's why we describe *principles and not formulas.* Managing stressors and getting in the Optimal Zone is as much an art as it is a science. We won't be prescribing recipes or specific protocols that apply equally to everyone. One size never has and never will fit all in biology or medicine. What may be a panacea for you could be a toxin for someone else. That's okay with us. Formulas are boring anyway. Principles are dynamic, flexible, and personal. They empower you to take charge in any situation and make the choices that are most likely to 1) minimize the negative consequences of stressors and 2) keep you in the optimal performance state.

So, if you see this as a journey rather than a destination, you'll set yourself up for a lifetime of adventure rather than a lifetime of feeling like a victim. You get to choose the direction. Survive or thrive—victim or victor—it is your choice.

WHAT PARTS OF YOUR BRAIN ARE YOU USING?

The human brain is a truly astounding structure of neural intricacy. You can think of it as being composed of three different layers: inner, middle, and outer. A basic understanding of each of these layers gives us a powerful and practical self-awareness. It helps us think strategically about how we respond to stressors, and it shows us better ways to respond through doing a little thinking of our own.

Inner Brain: Freeze and Seize

The inner brain, or *brain stem,* is found in all mammals, both low and high functioning. When danger flares, if swift action is not possible, the inner brain can automatically freeze us up. When a low-functioning organism confronts danger, their only option may be to shut down until the danger goes away or it is eaten. We humans may also automatically freeze up and lock down when faced with distressors. Depression is a behavioral manifestation of this shutting down. Procrastination, the fear of failure, holding back in withdrawal, and delayed reaction time can be manifestations of the stress response and the withdrawal reactions that come from the inner brain.

Middle Brain: Fight or Flight

The middle brain, or *diencephalon,* is found in higher-functioning animals. It works like a relay station for information that comes in from our senses. It compares that information with other information stored in our memory. When the middle brain puts all this information together and calculates that you are in some sort of danger (either real or perceived), it automatically kicks in the stress response to prepare you either to fight the danger or try to escape it. Some call this the reptilian response—*fight or flight.*

Outer Brain: Think and Choose

The outer brain, or *cerebral cortex*, gives more advanced creatures another brain layer—a higher level of input processing. This brain layer gives the organism many more options in its response to stressors because it can really think. The outer brain is highly developed in humans, giving us the capacity—*if* we choose—to ponder, choose, remember, imagine, predict, and make complex social and emotional decisions. In short, the cerebral cortex endows us with the ability to think things through and then make strategic choices. That's a huge advantage *if* you choose to do so. But we also have the other two layers. Sometimes withdrawal and doing nothing is okay if it's the best option until you can gather more information. In other words, you choose to do nothing rather than shut down involuntarily. Problems arise when you find yourself withdrawing when you should be acting, or when you act before engaging higher-processing brain areas enabling you to ponder other options.

Always aim to use the outer regions of your brain as much as possible so you can think more and react less. At times you might need to engage aggressively or run away. But it's always best if you can ponder the options first and reflect upon the various outcomes likely to be associated with the choices you are considering. When you do, you will be better equipped to select the option that will bring the best outcome—particularly when your plans and predictions get turned upside down.

That's what you've done by reading this book. You used your outer brain to make better choices in dealing with your stressors. Good decision.

The Challenge

When under distress, we revert to more primitive, inner parts of the brain. Rather than thinking logically, stressors seem to drive our decision-making inward, toward the part of the brain that tends to guide us by emotions, and down to the brain stem where we are simply reacting with no conscious thought at all.

As long as we experience minimal pressure, it's easy to remain in higher processing in the cerebral cortex. We consider all the options and share our ideas with others. Sometimes we advance to the action level and do what is appropriate for that way of thinking. But when the pressure really builds, we may begin to descend into feeling-based reactions in the diencephalon, or even reflexive responses controlled by the brain stem.

To stand in the Optimal Zone, you want one foot in higher processing so you can exercise good judgment; but you want the other in fight-or-flight mode so you can respond promptly. You want to access either of these areas quickly. This takes practice and some good solid mental work utilizing multiple brain areas—especially those associated with the prefrontal regions of the cerebral cortex. If you make it a habit to practice higher levels of thinking, when a major event happens, you're more likely to move up into that higher level of processing and reason through the situation.

OPTION B

Sheryl Sandberg served as the chief operating officer at Facebook. Before that, she was vice president of online sales at Google, and she had been the chief of staff at the US Department of the Treasury. She had two children she adored and a marriage that was dynamic, functional, and passionate. She spent most of her time in her Optimal Zone. She had achieved the ability to have balance in her life: balance between work and family, and balance between stress and recovery.

Then she experienced an intense amount of distress she could neither control nor could have predicted. Her world collapsed instantaneously when her husband Dave was found dead of a massive heart attack in the gym of the resort where they were vacationing.

Shock waves blasted through every area of her life. The ensuing tensions and pressures both crushed her and tore her apart. A few weeks after losing her husband, Sheryl was talking to one of her close confidants about an upcoming father-child activity. They had devised a plan for someone else to cover for her daughter's now-deceased father. But Sheryl cried, "I want Dave!" Her friend put his arm around her and said, "Option A is not available."[30] Even though Option B—life without Dave— wasn't what she wanted, her friend urged her to tackle her new reality head-on and use it as a time for learning and growth.

Thus began Sheryl's journey of letting go of the things she could not change and taking control of the ones she could. "We plant the seeds of resilience in the ways we process negative events," she wrote.[31] As Sheryl began facing her adversity, building resilience, and eventually finding joy, she relied on decades of research by people like psychologist Martin Seligman. Seligman has found that three beliefs can stall our recovery from intense distressors.

1. **Personalization**: The belief that we are the ones who are at fault for what has happened.

2. **Pervasiveness**: The belief that a stressor will affect all areas of our life.

3. **Permanence**: The belief that the effects of the stressor will last forever.

In contrast, Sheryl Sandberg was empowered when she realized we build resilience through four positive core beliefs.

1. I have considerable control over my life.

2. I can learn from failure.

3. I matter as a human being.

4. I have real strength I can rely on and share with others.[32]

We all have our ideals. Our dreams. Our plans for how life is supposed to work in our ideal world where we are in total control and can predict all stressors. The reality is that we live in a world where many stressors are uncontrollable and unpredictable.

TAKING CONTROL

Over the decades, the two of us have had the privilege of working with an incredible array of fantastic people functioning under some of the most intense stressors imaginable. Nick has worked in the life-and-death pressure cooker of international intelligence in addition to his research and immersion in the extreme endurance athletic world. Dick has had plenty of personal life stressors. As a pastor, a corporate executive, and now a personal coach for elite motorsport athletes, he clearly understands the realities of Option B.

Through these experiences, the two of us have discovered a handful of principles that make all the difference.

Key Principle #1: Manage What You Can Control

Key Principle #2: Go Slower to Go Faster

Key Principle #3: Look Farther Down the Track

Key Principle #4: Life Is Best When We Live for Something beyond Ourselves

Key Principle #1 is "Manage What You Can Control." It might sound simple, but complex research supports the idea that this is some of the best advice for finding and staying in your Optimal Zone. Too often we try to manage situations we can't control. For example, if I'm trying to be the perfect parent and I want my baby to sleep three hours without waking up, I'll feel like a failure when she is screaming and crying. If I'm a professional motorcycle racer, I might be riding at my personal best. But then a new hotshot performs off the charts in a particular race, and I don't know what to do to keep up with him. I feel as if I'm losing control. If I focus on *him*—whom I can't control—rather than on *me*—whom I can control—I'm going to get frustrated, start going slower, and making mistakes.

A couple of psychology terms relate to this.

⊙   *Internal locus of control* refers to the extent to which you feel in control of events.

⊙   *External locus of control* refers to the extent to which you feel events control you.

People scoring low on the internal locus of control measure believe they can do little to influence their outcomes. They adopt the posture of a victim and, when they act that way, it can become a self-fulfilling prophecy. A considerable body of research reveals that the feeling of helplessness, not the stressor, takes a toll on your health.

Some people surrender their sense of personal control by believing other people must always approve of their actions, or that they can never make mistakes, or that they can never be vulnerable. These beliefs ensure you will feel little control over major aspects of your life. By changing these beliefs and developing inner strength, you will find you face fewer out-of-control situations in life.

In circumstances that clearly *are* out of your control, you can use other approaches. Sometimes what is most helpful is to simply accept the fact that the situation is out of your hands. Let it go. People tend to labor over how to control a situation out of their control, which just makes them more upset. When you begin to feel anxious or distressed, that is probably the time to set the issue aside for a while and come back to it later.

If you do some thinking about control, you can even break a vicious cycle. Research shows that when you feel out of control, your stress levels increase. That increased stress can make you feel more out of control, again increasing your stress levels. Round and round the cycle goes. But you can break that cycle if you simply apply Key Principle #1 and *manage what you can control.* Merely perceiving you're in control can be effective, even if you can do little if anything to change the circumstances.[33] Being aware of your thoughts and taking control of what you can, lowers your stress. The reduced stress makes you feel as if you're more in control, which further lowers your stress.

"Life is really just an illustration for sports."

– UNKNOWN

Remember: if you always think about what you have always thought about, you will always feel what you have always felt. Instead:

- ⊙ Take charge of your life by taking control of your thoughts.

- ⊙ Learn to focus on what you can control.

- ⊙ Manage what you can control.

- ⊙ Remember, your attitude is within your control.

"The Serenity Prayer" can be one of the first steps to moving your life into the Optimal Zone where eustress and distress find their balance.

> *God, grant me the serenity*
> *To accept the things I cannot change,*
> *Courage to change the things I can,*
> *And wisdom to know the difference.*

We will unpack the other three key principles in the coming chapters.

NICK HALL: THE H₂O ZONE, PART 2

As we left the security of land behind, the winds filled our small sails and began to push our kayaks into the Gulf of Mexico. I became immediately aware of a growing nervousness—that tight feeling in your gut when the stress response starts to push adrenaline and cortisol into your system. I had always done these journeys solo or with one other person in my boat. Now I had two extra kayaks and three children under my watch.

The first day was not pleasant. The wind was in our faces, forcing us to tack back and forth across the wind to make forward progress in the open Gulf waters. Waves were crashing over the front of our boats, and we were taking on water. I diverted us toward the intracoastal waterway for a smoother but slower route. We still had hundreds of miles to go, and I began to worry that we wouldn't finish. My thoughts were consumed with the well-being of our team, and I became more and more aware that my control over their protection was limited.

That became real on Day 2 when my son-in-law, Joey, started to experience increasingly intense levels of pain from a sinus infection, particularly when his face was exposed to the sunlight. On the second day he was feeling so bad that we dropped him off on a dock where the owner of the house drove him to an emergency care clinic. In addition to the sinus infection, he was diagnosed with shingles. The doctor told him the pain would become excruciating and debilitating if he continued.

Joey had to withdraw from the Everglades Challenge.

It was a moment of reckoning for the whole team. I turned to Jackson, my thirteen-year-old grandson, and asked him, "Eagle (his Water Tribe name), do you think you can handle this boat and get it down to Key Largo?" He didn't hesitate. So I paired him with James (Swift), who had been in my boat. I powered my tandem boat solo. I was confident the boys could manage because Jackson had been doing the challenges with me since he was ten.

That night, as we sailed into the darkness to try to make up for lost time, the wind was strong and the seas were heavy. All I could see through the darkness was the light on their kayak. But I could hear chatter and laughter coming from their boat. "Whoo! Whoo!" They had figured out how to surf their boat down the waves. Perhaps this was all going to work out after all.

After a few hours of sleep on a remote wind-swept beach, we were ready to go again when a wind advisory went out for small craft, along with a wind chill advisory as temperatures were dropping down into the low 40s. My plan was to hurry south to an island off Fort Myers where we could make camp on the leeward side and sit out the storm. More hard sailing into the growing winds, more and more waves crashing over the bows, and I had thirteen- and twelve-year-old boys out there alone in their boat.

During Day 4, my radio crackled to life. It was Eagle. "Pelican! I just saw a sailboat capsize. It looks like three people are in the water. Should we go help?" We were the only boats around. "Absolutely," I replied. I had a small VHF handheld radio with a very short antenna. I tried to radio for emergency support but had no response. We were out of range. Then I sent Julie and Abigail to shore to summon help for when we would eventually get there—with the three survivors of the capsized sailboat, we hoped.

By the time we got to the capsized boat, the situation was dire: three elderly men, struggling in the waves and suffering deeply from the cold. I focused on the one who appeared most tired and distressed. I tried to pull him onto my boat, but it was impossible.

"I don't even have the strength to hold on. Better just let me go," he said. "Don't worry about me. Go for the others."

"Listen! You have got to hang on for one more minute! Just one more minute!" I shouted into his hopeless eyes. He agreed, clinging to the side of my kayak. I grabbed the anchor line and knotted it around his chest. (The irony of this escaped me at that moment. Tying an anchor onto a drowning man? Something you might see in The Sopranos or The Godfather.) I was able to get a seat cushion from the capsized boat and put that under his head to keep it above water as I tied him to my kayak. He was safe for the moment.

Now what about the other two? When I turned around to retrieve them, the two were already sitting on Jackson and James's boat, safe and sound. But how? Without any instruction, the boys had masterfully maneuvered their kayak up onto the exposed centerboard of the capsized boat, creating a step for the remaining two gentlemen to step down onto their small boat. Thirteen- and twelve-year-olds... a combination of common sense and competence in a life-or-death situation. They had it.

We headed for the distant beach: Eagle and Swift seriously overloaded with the two extra men, me dragging the third one through the waves. We were met on the beach by EMTs and the Marine patrol who had been summoned by Julie and Abigail. Everyone played a critical role, including Julie (Kite) and eleven-year-old Abbey (Sparrow). A delightful couple vacationing in a nearby house offered coffee and comfort.

As soon as possible after repairing some rescue-related damage, we launched again, trying to make up for more lost time by running through the night. Before setting out at the start, I *had made up my mind I was not going to do any serious night sailing. But we had no choice if we were going to finish on time.*

That made me very nervous, particularly for the safety of the children. They would often take naps in the back of the boat. With the two boys alone in their boat and as small as they were, I was concerned about them literally falling out. Though they were only a few yards away, it still seemed like a long distance; in the wind it was hard to get their attention. We used whistles. We had flare guns. Also, each person was equipped with an EPIRB (an emergency transmitter and locator beacon) that would summon the Coast Guard with the press of a button. Each boat was also equipped with a satellite transponder so family, friends, and Water Tribe officials could get updates of our exact position every five to ten minutes. We also use the waterproof marine radios to stay in constant communication. But still, when all I could see was that little dot of light on the back of their boat, I was worried and watched them like a hawk.

We pressed on this way for two more days and nights. Then, at about midnight on Day 7, Jackson's voice crackled over the radio. "Pelican, we're taking on water!" In the dark we assessed the situation. The boat had been damaged during the rescue and was leaking. I tried to come up with a solution. Option A had evaporated. Option B had failed. And after considering every possibility I brokenheartedly concluded we had no Option C.

Winston Churchill is famous for saying, "Never give in. Never give in. Never, never, never, never. In nothing, great or small, large or petty. Never give in—except to convictions of honor and good sense." In our situation, good sense prevailed; it was time to head to the shore and call it quits. We had come so far and were so close. Now we would only be listed as DNF, Did Not Finish.

We located the car and trailer my wife had left for us at the ranger station in the Everglades, packed up, and drove to Key Largo, having fallen short of our goal. We had failed to reach the finish line. I did my best to buffer their discouragement, but I sounded like a beat-up coach after a tough loss.

But by the time we got to Key Largo, word had spread about what had happened with the rescue. At the awards ceremony Jackson and James were given standing ovations and a special award. Two Scout Masters from the Water Tribe were there and insisted Jackson and James be nominated for the rare Boy Scouts of America Hero Award. The two men they saved both agreed to write letters on their behalf.

We also received a very nice letter from the eighty-nine-year-old gentleman I had towed to the beach. He sent a beautiful metal sculpture of the DNA double helix. It turns out he's the artist commissioned to create these double helix models for the Nobel Laureate James Watson who discovered the structure of DNA. "The structure of DNA is the essence of life," he wrote. "I feel it is an appropriate gift to give you for saving mine."

Looking back, I can't help but think that our entire team had just experienced a pinnacle of the Optimal Zone. In an onslaught of stressors I could have neither predicted nor controlled, I had been part of a team that responded with everything they could control. Because of it, three families still had their grandpas. And I can't help but think that two boys became young men along the way

"Everything can be taken from a man but one thing: the last of human freedoms—to choose one's attitude in any given set of circumstances, to choose one's own way."

— VIKTOR FRANKL

DEATH TO VICTIMIZATION

Your journey through life is a lot like extreme endurance sports events. Reality shows little respect for our hopes and expectations. Real-life stressors, many of them intense and long lasting, are part of the journey. You'll encounter sickness, loss, storms, shattered relationships, and long, cold nights of the soul. And while these stressors may feel personal, pervasive, and permanent, you *can* always control your thoughts and your attitude.

Yes, the lower-functioning levels of your brain may make you feel helpless and out of control. But by using the power of higher processing, you can embrace Option B. Or C or D. Yes, choices must be made. In the face of uncontrollable and unpredictable stressors, you can roll over and play the victim if you want to. Or your stressors can be harnessed and managed for a greater good.

We believe the most powerful tool you can harness is to *manage what you can control*. In fact, managing what you can control is the *only* option you have. And you might even be able to use it to help people in real need along the way.

That's what Part 2 is all about—tools for managing

stressors and using them to get in the Optimal Zone for your benefit as well as those around you.

CHAPTER 3 TAKEAWAYS

Into the Zone

- ⊙ Some stressors you can control and predict.

- ⊙ Some stressors you can neither control nor predict.

- ⊙ Any given stressor has an optimal range of intensity in any given person, any given situation, at any given time. It is the *Optimal Zone*.

Too Hot? Too Cold? Just Right!

Excessive high-intensity stressors can result in distress; so can chronic low levels of stressors. Aim for optimal stressor intensities.

- ⊙ Introduce eustress where needed.

- ⊙ Reduce distress when possible.

What Parts of Your Brain Are You Using?

- ⊙ The brain stem controls involuntary systems and reactions.

- ⊙ The diencephalon is the emotional center of the brain that adds a level of feeling.

- The cerebral cortex is the thinking outer layer of brain tissue that allows us to gather, process, and make conscious decisions.

- In order to manage stressors, always aim for higher brain processes through conscious decisions, and by all means be aware of what you are thinking about.

Option B

Life *never* unfolds as we plan. We become victims if we buy into three negative beliefs.

- **Personalization:** The belief that we are the ones who are at fault for all that has happened

- **Pervasiveness:** The belief that a stressor in one area of our lives will affect all areas of our lives

- **Permanence:** The belief that the effects of the stressor will last forever

Resiliency is empowered through four positive core beliefs.

- I have considerable control over my life.

- I can learn from failure.

- I matter as a human being.

- I have real strength I can rely on and share with others.[34]

To find serenity and balance:

- ⊙ Accept the things you cannot change.

- ⊙ Have courage to change the things you can.

- ⊙ Seek wisdom to know the difference.

Death to Victimization

With knowledge comes new responsibility. We are now responsible for choosing between being a victim or being a victor in the journey of life. It's time to manage what we can control—our thoughts and attitudes that will empower us to manage our stressors for the good of all.

STRESS RECOVERY IN ATHLETES

Where the Rubber Meets the Road

Dick Tibbits

e know that the principles contained in the Stress Recovery program work on individuals, but can they help world-class professional athletes improve their performance? I set out to test that idea with the athletes I work with across a wide range of sports. For this particular paper I will focus on one of the oldest racing sports in our country: American Flat Track motorcycle racing.

These riders race on oval dirt circles, often on horse tracks or dirt stock car ovals. They simply go fast, turn left, and repeat. They can attain speeds of up to 135 miles per hour on the mile tracks and then pitch the bike sideways to scuff speed and slide through the turns. They have no front brakes to slow themselves down and, if that were not enough to feel your heart in your chest, they are often within inches of each other as they enter the turn. Some call it the greatest show on earth.

My job in working with these world premier professional racers is to help them stay calm and focused in the midst of the pressure cooker called racing. There are thousands of dollars on the line depending on how they finish. The major motorcycle manufacturers are there along with large corporations that sponsor these riders. These "kids"—ages sixteen to thirty—have a lot of pressure to perform. And if they don't, they could lose their ride at the end of the season.

You have heard the expression that at the top of any sport, what separates the best from the rest is often mental. While each athlete must have the skills and fitness to perform at the highest level of their sport, it is the mental toughness demonstrated by the winners that makes the final difference between winning and losing.

So how do I help these riders achieve the success they desire? I will share a case study with the last six riders I worked with. I will not share individual data, for as in any sport, confidentiality and personal performance tips between riders is secretive. No one wants to give away their competitive advantage. So by presenting composite data on all six riders, the individual differences and approaches each rider uses is protected.

Let me start at the beginning. Before I start working with a racer I collect baseline data so we can monitor and improve performance based on objective feedback rather than personal opinion. I use heart rate as a measure of stress because heart rate responds most dramatically to either:

movement/exercise and thoughts/feelings. So the harder you work, the higher your heart rate will rise. But it is equally as true, the more stress you experience, the higher your heart rate rises. So if I know what a rider's heart rate is, based upon repeated measurement of how much physical effort is required to do a task when it is just practice and there is little pressure to perform, and then compare that to their heart rate when competing in a national event, the difference in heart rates will be attributable primarily to stress. And in fact, that proves to be true.

The average heart rate when each rider was pushing it as hard and fast as they could on a practice track was between the high 150s and lower 160s. Yet on race day their average heart rate was in the mid-190s. Same effort doing the same thing, with the same speeds on practice day, yet their heart rate increase by over 30 beats a minute. That is the measure of stress they experience because of the pressure they face to perform not only at their best, but better than anyone else that day.

Why is this important? There is a saying in racing that you have to go slower in order to go faster. What that means is if you are pushing it too hard, you are more likely to make mistakes, and you simply can't go as fast unless you are smooth into the turns. So does that mean they actually have to go slower on the track? Of course not; how can you win doing that! What it does mean is that they have to slow things down on the inside of their mind. And my measure for that inner calm is heart rate.

After training with me based on the principles in the

Stress Recovery program, the riders were able to compete at the highest level, with improved results, and with a heart rate in the upper 160s to mid-170s on race day. How were they able to do this?

While my approach to each rider is highly individualized, there are certain things I do consistently with each rider. First, I improve their endurance by doing weekly one hour to one and a half hours on a bicycle ride with their heart rate close to the anaerobic threshold. This is where your body goes from aerobic (able to carry enough oxygen to fuel your muscles) to anaerobic (where your muscles are having to work oxygen deprived). This way their body develops optimal endurance so they are not expending as much energy, compared to before, to do the same amount of work. This helps lower the heart rate, because the demands of the muscles are not as great, for they are now more efficient.

But we also have to train the body to recover, which is what we teach in the Stress Recovery program. You can take on more stress when you learn to balance that stress with great recovery. So yes, you guessed it, I have them doing interval training. This is where they get their heart rate up to a certain point and immediately stop, so we can measure how long it takes for heart rate to recover to a lower threshold. For example, I have them do a series of six intervals where they take their heart rate up to 170 and then drop it down to 120 before repeating the cycle all over again. I then measure how long it takes the heart rate to drop those 50 beats a minute.

Initially it would take anywhere from 60 to 90 seconds for the heart rate to drop from 170 to 120. But after practice, each athlete I worked with was able to achieve that drop in heart rate in under 30 seconds. That is amazing and is only achieved by the top athletes. But you can also improve your recovery rate and measure that improvement in the same way. You may only want to take your heart rate up to 150 then drop it down to 100. That works and you will still get the training effect of improved recovery. Try it for yourself; it works. Just be patient with yourself; it may take a month or two to see real results.

Why is it important that you train your body to recover quickly? Because you want your body doing this automatically—outside of your awareness. You are training a cardiovascular response that every time your heart rate goes up, it can be expected to go down. And the more ingrained this pathway, the quicker the response.

Another thing I noticed when working with these athletes is that while sitting around in the pits, waiting for the next race to start, they would have a heart rate ranging from the upper 90s to 110 beats per minute. This is high for just sitting around in a chair. So again, there are two factors driving heart rate: activity and stress. If there is no activity, they are just sitting and waiting, then you can be pretty confident stress is building. And it is building without the athletes realizing they are stressed. The same can happen to you. Stress often builds throughout the day, and we are not even aware of its impact. After all, it's not just the big events that stress; many little stressors can be just as dangerous.

There are two ways I help athletes reduce stress, which are the same things we teach in our Stress Recovery program.

They need to practice deep breathing, and they need to do progressive muscle relaxation. These two techniques are explained in this book, so I will not repeat how that is done. What I do want to share with you, as a result of the racers using these techniques, is the results.

After working with a racer utilizing these two techniques (while I use more than these two techniques depending on the racer, I always use at least these two proven approaches to heart rate reduction), their normal heart rate while sitting in the pits is now in the mid-60s. What a difference. They are no longer expending all that energy for no useful purpose. And they are staying calm under pressure. In fact, with practice, when I have a racer lie down and just rest their mind from all the thoughts racing through their head and breathe slowly and deeply, they are able to get their heart rate down into the low 50s and upper 40s on race day. They were never able to do that before. What an advantage over their competition in terms of controlling the nerves and conserving energy.

In addition to race day heart rate I also have the athletes checking their heart rate throughout the day at home to make sure they are managing their stress and staying calm in the midst of all the chaos that can happen on a daily basis in their lives. Probably not much different than your life. One of the numbers I have them monitor is their resting heart rate, which is taken first thing in the morning before they get out of bed. This really sets the bottom end of your heart rate. All of the riders I work with, after following the principles of the Stress Recovery Effect, succeed in achieving resting heart rates in the 40s. I have one athlete whose resting heart rate is in the upper 30s. You don't need to get that low, but it demonstrates that by working the program contained in this book, you too can achieve remarkable results.

So this is all well and good, but does it make a difference in performance? To prove that it does, I will take an average of where these six racers were in the points standings the year before I started working with them and compare that to where they stood on average at the end of the race year in which I worked with them. The average place in the point standing for these six riders the year before I worked with them was seventh place. The average place in the point standings at the end of the year I worked with them was second place, with two of the riders I worked with winning the grand national championship the first year we worked together. That is a major accomplishment, considering how competitive the sport is.

Two riders Dick coaches – 69, 44 – lead the race (Credit: Dave Hoenig, Flat Trak Fotos)

What works for these athletes will also work for you. Stay with the program and you will notice that it is not the amount of stress you face day to day, but rather how quickly you can recover from that stress and move on. You will find yourself having more energy and being more calm in the midst of all the things that go on around you. It works as demonstrated with the six athletes I worked with over the last several years.

PART 2

EQUIPPING STRATEGIES

"Resilience is not a fixed personality trait.
It's a lifelong project."
—SHERYL SANDBERG

We blended up a mixture of science and experience in Part 1. The scientific method gives us powerful raw data from which to learn, but experience is still the best teacher. Unquestionably, you have plenty of experiences of your own—some good and some not so good, and some that will change the course of your life for better or worse. Managing stressors is an important part of living a successful life. Let's start working on how you manage your stress.

In Part 2 you'll roll up your sleeves and start building a better life on the foundational principles you learned in Part 1. You'll begin to take control of your own stress management for a better life all around.

Part 1 was all about:

Key Principle #1: Manage What You Can Control

The simplicity of that principle is empowered when you use the amazing outer regions of your brain. It's one of the primary truths that leads us into a healthy management of our stressors. And the corollary to this principle is *don't try to manage what you can't control.* This futile effort only increases your stressors and frustration.

Part 2 is all about:

Key Principle #2: Go Slower to Go Faster

You're probably thinking, *Really? Go slower to go faster?* It's true. When you slow things down on the inside, you have a lot more energy and focus to get more done. This will make sense to you shortly.

Imagine Part 2 of this book as an old toolbox—like the one your grandfather may have had in his garage. Open the lid and you'll see a top tray with tools in it. Pull out that tray and you find more tools in the bottom. The top tray has the tools Grandpa needed immediately or in an emergency. Pliers, hammer, screwdriver, roll of duct tape, etc. That's what he used to *fix* things. In the bottom were tools to *build* things. Wrenches, sockets, saws, hardware, a tape measure, etc.

Think of the next two chapters as your *Stressor-Management Toolbox*. Chapter 4 is your top tray and contains *Response Strategies* for immediate repairs. Chapter 5 is the bottom of the toolbox and contains *Lifestyle Strategies* for building better things.

Response Strategies are *intervention* strategies you can use immediately or in an emergency when you're facing high acute stress. They help you regain and/or maintain control when your stress response has been triggered. They also reduce the negative symptoms of stressors.

The seven Response Strategies are:

1. **Breathe It Out:** Responding to Stressors One Breath at a Time

2. **Stretch It:** Flexing to Avoid Snapping

3. **Let It Go:** Tensing Up to Wind Down

4. **Act It Out:** Do It to Feel It

5. **Pause It:** Buying Time for Better Choices

6. **Rock It:** Swaying Away the Stressors

7. **Laugh It Up:** Laughter Is Still the Best Medicine

We will show you how and when to best use these seven tools in chapter 4. With practice you'll begin to reach *automatically* for the right tools anytime a situation seems to be going to pieces. With practice these tools will tap into the power of your brain. The objective is to train your brain to respond to immediate stressors in a way that gets you out of the excessive distress zone as quickly as possible. It's the Optimal Zone of eustress we are after—that place where we can perform in a healthy, productive, and creative way. Remember, *performance* has a broad meaning in this book; we are talking about *all* aspects of life.

Lifestyle Strategies are tools that will keep you from the extremes of distress in the first place. Remember the Optimal Zone: not too hot and not too cold; you want to always aim for just right. While the upper tray contains *intervention* strategies, the lower part of your toolbox contains *prevention* strategies.

The seven Lifestyle Strategies are:

1. **Think About It:** Engaging Your Outer Brain for the Better

2. **Sense It:** Creating Environmental Eustress

3. **Reduce It:** Cutting Stressors Off at the Source

4. **Forgive It:** Finding Freedom from the Past

5. **Move It:** Exercise Always Wins the Day

6. **Eat It Up:** Ingesting the Good Stuff

7. **Give It a Rest:** Taking Intentional Breaks for Ultimate Performance

We will show you how to use these seven tools over time to reduce the chronic nature of distressors and leverage eustress to your advantage in chapter 5.

By the end of Part 2 of this book, you'll have a complete toolbox.

- ⊙ Seven Response Strategies in your top tray for immediate and emergency repairs.

- ⊙ (Think *intervention* when you think "Response Strategy.")

- ⊙ Seven Lifestyle Strategies in the bottom of your toolbox to build a new future.

- ⊙ (Think *prevention* when you think "Lifestyle Strategy.")

You've already started using two of the tools in the breathing and tense-and-release activities. We will revisit these tools so you can discover the science behind why they work so well. Then we will explore the other tools. Along the way you'll discover what the *go slower to go faster* principle is all about.

Does this program truly work for real people? Listen to what one participant said who went through *The Stress Recovery Effect* program held at AdventHealth (formerly Florida Hospital) in Orlando, Florida:

I learned so much about how stress has affected me physically and emotionally in ways I never understood. It actually helped me not feel so much like a failure but rather realize that stress has really impacted me adversely. And I even mean going back fifty-plus years ago. I can interpret better now things I experienced. This was so very valuable!

So welcome to Part 2.

Let's pick up some tools and start building a better life!

CHAPTER 4

RESPONSE STRATEGIES

Tools to Help in the Moment

DICK TIBBITS: A MATTER OF THE HEART

A s a motor sports trainer, I get to work with some fascinating people—motorcycle racers and race car drivers—who make their living by pushing the extreme limits of both man and machine. I know these are unusual people, but at the core they're just like each of us. Their stressors might seem extreme, but their brains and bodies react just like ours when we face stressors in everyday life. Financial struggles? Someone cuts you off in traffic? Teenager on the edge? Blow-up with your spouse? We are all in the same boat.

I also get to work with some really fun technology. I work with a heart rate monitoring company called Polar. By way of Bluetooth, I connect the racers' Polar heart monitors to my iPad. While everyone else is watching the racers on the outside, I can watch what's going on in their insides. When they come off the track, I can pop up their heart rates on my iPad and see exactly what their heart rate was doing at certain places on the track. Does their heart rate climb when someone tries to pass them? How do they react when they are way out in front? I can analyze it all.

Heart Rate Variation Under Pressure

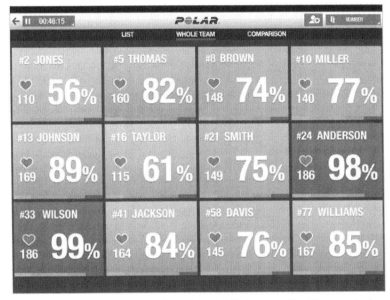

Courtesy of Polar, used with permission

Why is this important? Because at any given moment on the track, an optimal heart rate keeps each racer in the Optimal Zone. Heart rate too low? They aren't pushing as hard as they need to in order to win. Heart rate too high? They are more likely to make a mistake because they are running on adrenaline and they won't have anything in reserve for an emergency. The same is true for all of us.

When I first started working in motorcycle racing, I went around to the different racers and checked their heart rates.

What I noticed was, even when they were simply "standing around" in the pits, hours before they would head out on the track to race, all their heart rates were in the range of 100–120 beats per minute (BPM). I thought, That's pretty high for hanging out doing nothing. *(A normal resting heart rate in a healthy, relaxed person is about 60–70 BPM.)*

One day I was tracking the heart rate of one particular racer, who was simply relaxing in his chair, when a mechanic started a motorcycle he was tuning. I noticed the racer's heart rate jumped significantly—up into the 130–140 BPM range. Interesting, *I thought.* Just the sound of a motorcycle is enough to increase his stress response; and he's still not racing. *By the time a racer gets to the starting line they could be up to 170 BPM. By the time they get the green light, they're not too far from their maximum heart rate. At that point, they are certainly going to be pushed out of their Optimal Performance Zone, become quickly exhausted, and start making mistakes. Now you can understand when they say, "For the top performers, it is all mental." These unnecessarily fast heart rates were slowing them down on the track. I needed to teach them to go slower to go faster. I will teach you the same principle as well.*

WE'VE GOT THE BEAT

Every one of us is in a race of our own making in this modern world. We've come to call life the "rat race" for good reason—no, not because you're a rat, but because life can seem like an endless spinning around in a wheel that goes nowhere. The physiological and mental stressors can push our heart rates well out of the Optimal Performance Zone. Sure, we may never strap ourselves into a race car or launch a dirt bike dozens of feet into the air, but we can feel the all-pervasive stressors that bombard us from all sides. Distress from chronic stress response (too much for too long) or a sedentary, lethargic life (too little for too long) causes us to feel stressed out.

A heart rate monitor can also show you what's going on inside your body beat by beat. This is a form of biofeedback that lets you observe what is going on inside your body when you can't always feel it. Having this information can be a real motivator to start managing what you can see and control. You can pick up a relatively inexpensive heart rate monitor and start tracking your heart rate today. You don't need the best or most accurate monitor, just something that will show you your approximate heart rate and how it changes throughout the day. First, let's look at how you can control heart rate in the moment.

You can control heart rate by:

1. Doing something

2. Thinking something

We all know that if you start running, your heart rate will go up and, conversely, if you stop running and sit down for a while, your heart rate will come down. But did you know that if you think about someone or something unpleasant, your heart rate will go up? And if you think about something you enjoy, like relaxing on the beach, your heart rate will go down? And this can all happen while you are sitting still.

The seven *intervention* "Response Strategies" are tools you can use to *do* something and *think* something right now—in the moment—to move you out of the zone of extreme distress. For example, imagine you're in charge of a committee that has been tasked with resolving a conflict. Everyone in the room agrees what the conflict is as they share their thoughts about how best to resolve it. Everyone works together with no hidden agendas to achieve the goal.

But now a looming deadline adds pressure. Furthermore, some members of the committee push for one solution over another—but not because it's best for the organization, but because they will derive some personal gain. You're in charge and realize the bickering will cause you to miss the deadline. That's when you take over and proclaim a decision must be made right now. "If it turns out to be a mistake, we'll fix it later." The deadline causes you to take immediate action without carefully thinking through the consequences.

Now others in the group feel pressure too. They begin distorting their arguments and/or deliberately leaving out valuable information in order to achieve their personal agenda. The level of conflict has escalated to the highest level; it is so intense people have forgotten what the initial issue was. Some people may even want to see you fail for purely vindictive and selfish reasons. Under the escalating pressure, your stress level rises to the point where you throw your hands up in despair and angrily tell the group you're not taking this anymore as you storm out of the room.

Now the situation has become a lose-lose scenario for everyone. In hindsight, you can learn an important lesson from this example. People change under stress, sometimes switching from a position grounded in reason to one fueled by raw emotion. You've undoubtedly been there, whether in the boardroom, the classroom, or at home. Stressors that go unmanaged in the moment can have catastrophic consequences.

Let's examine each one of the seven Response Strategies and explore the powerful ways you can intervene and manage stressors for your own good and the benefit of all. The remainder of this chapter will give you seven powerful tools for managing stress to your advantage in the moment.

RESPONSE STRATEGY #1: BREATHE IT OUT

Responding to Stressors One Breath at a Time

What It Is

Controlled, deep breathing is one of the simplest and most effective strategies you can use to cope more effectively with stressors. Controlled breathing:

- ⊙ Enables you to focus better

- ⊙ Establishes an optimal level of oxygen in your body

- ⊙ Induces a feeling of being in control. You will almost immediately feel better because you are actively doing something. And remember, it's not the stressor but your feeling of helplessness that is detrimental to you, so any sense of control is your friend

⊙ Allows you to distance yourself mentally from the immediate stressor through a choice you control

Why It Works for You

Breathing influences your blood gasses, which in turn affect heart rate. You cannot consciously control the proportions of oxygen and carbon dioxide in your blood, but you can regulate your breathing and, in doing so, transmit signals throughout the body which have the ultimate effect of stabilizing various physiological systems.

The Science Behind It

The rapid and shallow breathing often associated with fear and anxiety can create a buildup of carbon dioxide (CO_2) in the bloodstream. Carbon dioxide is a by-product of metabolism. As the body prepares to activate the fight-or-flight response, metabolism increases, which increases CO_2 levels. Some of the CO_2 is converted into carbonic acid, a waste product, which compounds the problem. The brain detects the higher levels of CO_2 and acidity, which will result in more rapid and deeper breathing to restore the balance between life-giving oxygen and the waste product. At the same time your muscles tense, metabolism increases even more, and the levels of CO_2 continue to build despite the brain's efforts to restore harmony.

This is the perfect recipe for anxiety! Elevated CO_2 has been directly correlated with attacks of anxiety. Thus, while the anxious state occurred in *response* to something threatening in the environment, the emotional state of anxiety is *perpetuated* by the physiological consequences of increased metabolism.

When you are unable to control your fear, start by taking control of your breathing. This technique establishes optimal levels of oxygen in your body, which soothes the nerves and enables you to think more clearly, making you better prepared to deal with your feelings and their cause. But, more importantly, controlled breathing brings CO_2 back into a range that won't escalate anxiety.

For added benefit, breathe in through your nose and out through your mouth. How does this help? Inside your nose is a labyrinth of nasal passages. (You become aware of this in a bad way when you have a cold and your nose stuffs up. The passages get filled with mucus and make breathing difficult.) These membranes have an important function. Think of them as the radiator for your brain. When air passes over the radiator of your car, the engine is cooled; as air passes through your nasal passages, the adjacent part of your brain is cooled. That part of your brain happens to be the frontal lobe, which plays a pivotal role in your decisions and interpretation of emotions. When the outside air is cooler than your body temperature, each inhalation through your nose results in cooling air passing through your nasal passages, thereby maintaining an optimal temperature in the brain's frontal lobes. Keep in mind that when cells, including neurons, become more active, one by-product is heat. Of course, on a frigid day, the same passageways can warm the air before it enters the lungs. So the next time you feel the temperature rising as you get more and more upset, use controlled breathing to calm yourself and cool down.

Perhaps that's why long before the brain was understood, expressions suggesting a correlation between emotionality and heat were common. "Don't be so hot-headed," "cool your jets," and "feeling the heat" are some examples. Controlling your breathing is an indirect means by which to exert control over many physiological processes! Equally important is the fact that you experience the benefits of controlled breathing almost immediately, reinforcing your belief that you are not helpless. The simple act of taking control can, by itself, be therapeutic.

How to Do It

The body associates deep breathing with a state of relaxation. If you feel panic setting in, breathe deeply; relax with each inhale and let the fear go. Here are some steps introduced in Part 1 to get you started.

- ⊙ Sit up straight or lie down if possible.

- ⊙ Put your hands to your sides or rest them on your thighs.

- ⊙ Slowly inhale through your nose.

- ⊙ When you inhale, imagine your stomach to be a balloon you are blowing up until full. You can even put your hands gently on your stomach to feel it rise and fall.

- ⊙ While extending your stomach outward, fill your chest, and then expand all the way up to your shoulders.

- ⊙ Hold the full breath for a count of three.

- ⊙ Let all the air out slowly through your mouth. Your exhale should be about one-third longer than your inhale. The reason for this is that maximum relaxation occurs on the exhale.

- ⊙ It is helpful to breathe in through your nose and out through your mouth.

Even a single breath is going to help. Take four to six breaths like this and you will really feel the difference.

And there it is! Your first tool in the top tray of your toolbox is a simple, powerful Response Strategy. You can do it anywhere and anytime—and it's only a breath away.

RESPONSE STRATEGY #2: STRETCH IT
Flexing to Avoid Snapping

What It Is

Stretching is as simple as it sounds: Take some part of your body and move it in a way that gently extends your muscles and tendons while also fortifying the joints beneath those muscles and tendons. Metaphorically, *stretching* might prevent you from *snapping* physically, mentally, or emotionally. In the next chapter, we will examine stretching as part of an exercise program that creates a healthier lifestyle that will prevent you from experiencing chronic stress responses. For now, though, let's look at how stretching can be used as an *intervention* strategy when your stress response is already kicking in.

"Stressed muscles are tight, tense muscles. By learning to relax your muscles, you will be able to use your body to dissipate stress."[35] —HARVARD HEALTH

Why It Works for You

Stretching produces good results for your body and brain.

- ⊙ Increases flexibility

- ⊙ Increases your range of motion

- ⊙ Improves blood flow to your muscles

⊙ Improves posture and body alignment

⊙ Helps to heal your body

⊙ Relieves pain

⊙ Improves your performance and reduces risk of injury

A word of caution: don't try to overstretch, as you could cause more damage than good.

Stretching doesn't only help your body physiologically. It also helps your brain psychologically.

⊙ Simply making a choice can help reduce stress. When you stretch, you are choosing to do something. Making that decision and acting on it helps get your brain moving in the right direction.

⊙ Taking action increases your sense of self-control. We talked about this concept at the end of Part 1. It's very important you know you *can* take actions that will help. Stretching is one of those you can do that will help you. The sense of control can lead to a chain reaction of better thinking.

How to Do It

Start in either a standing or sitting position. If you can get outside to do this activity, all the better.

⊙ Place your arms at your sides with your fingers gently being drawn by gravity toward the floor.

⊙   Breathe, using several controlled breaths.

⊙   Reach for the sky. Swing your arms upward until all your fingers are pointing toward the ceiling or sky and your elbows are straight.

⊙   Look up. Gently tilt your head back until you are looking through your hands at the ceiling or sky. Feel the stretch.

⊙   Rock it. Reach as high as you can with one hand and then reach as high as you can with the other. Do this back and forth a couple of times, feeling the stretch.

⊙   Breathe a couple of times.

⊙   Draw in a big breath through your nose and slowly exhale through your mouth as you slowly lower your hands to your side.

⊙   Smile! You are doing something good for yourself.

⊙   Now let's head in the other direction.

⊙   Start either sitting or standing.

⊙   Straighten up as if someone were gently lifting up on your head.

⊙   Place your arms at your side with your fingers gently being drawn by gravity toward the floor.

⊙   Breathe, using several controlled breaths.

⊙   Keeping your back fairly straight, slowly and

gently reach for your toes as far as you comfortably can.

- ⊙ While you are bent over, draw in a couple of slow, deep breaths.

- ⊙ Tilt your head toward your chest and slowly roll back to an upright position.

- ⊙ Repeat four to six times.

- ⊙ Smile again! You are taking control.

Even just a few stretches will help. If you do several repetitions slowly and smoothly with controlled breaths, you'll feel the tension lift and the frantic feelings calm down.

Not every tool in the box will fix everything completely. A good stretch may not be a cure, but it can certainly be one of the tools that helps a lot. Let's keep examining more options.

 ## RESPONSE STRATEGY #3: LET IT GO
Tensing Up to Wind Down

What It Is

Progressive muscle relaxation is a technique that has brought stress recovery worldwide. We introduced this idea at the end of chapter 2 so you could immediately apply it. Now we are going to build out this technique so you understand why it works so well and expand on the concept so you can maximize its positive effects.

In short, this recovery strategy involves:

⊙ Smoothly tightening specific muscles in a controlled way

⊙ Slowly relaxing those muscles into a calmer, stronger state.

Why It Works for You

Progressive muscle relaxation is a process of tension followed by relaxation, which is a way to train the body to balance stress (tension) with recovery (relaxation). The tension is beneficial when it's preparing you for a burst of speed, but when it continues in anticipation of a threat that is unlikely to materialize, the continuing stress response can wreak havoc on your body, as we described earlier. Progressive muscle relaxation works in part because it imposes an interlude of recovery. You can think of it as an anti-stressor.

⊙ Research has shown that people who use progressive muscle relaxation can:

⊙ Reduce their heart rate, blood pressure, and anxiety

⊙ Experience greater blood flow throughout their body along with a sense of calmness

⊙ Activate or increase the production of opiates (natural relaxants)

⊙ Optimize immunities, making them more resilient to illnesses

Because some kinds of stress can negatively impact your reaction time, your immune system's ability to fight illness, and your memory, you may well experience benefits in these abilities as well.[36]

How to Do It

Like the other Response Strategies, every little bit will help. To get the full effect, simply keep building on what you've started. With a little practice, you'll discover you can do this strategy in almost any situation and in almost any posture.

- ⊙ For about ten to fifteen seconds, tense a particular muscle group until you feel discomfort. Make yourself aware of that discomfort.

- ⊙ Then, over the same time frame, relax the same muscles as you become aware of the pleasant sensation associated with the relaxation.

- ⊙ Imagine the tension literally draining from your muscles during the relaxation phase.

It's up to you how to progress, but typically a person will start with the hands and wrists, proceed to the arms, shoulders, and then chest, before progressing to the stomach, thighs, calves, and feet. Don't forget your neck, eyes, and scalp!

Plan to spend from ten to thirty minutes doing this (depending on how many you do and how long you do each exercise). You can combine progressive muscle relaxation with the same breathing techniques already described.

Avoid allowing intrusive thoughts to interfere. Creating

a conditioned stimulus may help. Choose a calming word or phrase, which you will recite each time you exhale and release the muscle tension. After a while, the phrase will acquire the same properties that Pavlov's bell did after the sound was paired with the sight and smell of meat.

Later, in the absence of the conscious effort to relax, reciting the word or phrase alone will help reduce your anxiety and get you back on track.

Remember, one size doesn't fit all. It's also important to take control. So customize the process in whatever way works best for you. Perhaps you have enough tension already, so eliminate that part if it's best for you. Instead of a word or phrase, use a fragrance or music to precede the relaxation phase. Follow the basic process but make it yours.

To familiarize yourself with this process, start by lying comfortably on your back.

⊙ Take a deep breath and hold it.

⊙ Slowly make fists and gently increase the pressure until your hands and lower arms are firmly tensed.

⊙ While slowly exhaling, leisurely let your hands go limp again. (Remember that, as a general principle, the relaxation always comes on the exhale.)

⊙ Shake your hands loosely, as if the tension is flowing out onto the floor.

⊙ Take two more complete, deep breaths.

⊙ Rest a moment.

Then move to other muscle groups. The University of Michigan Health System suggests the following list:[37]

MUSCLE GROUP	WHAT TO DO
Hands	Clench them.
Wrists and forearms	Extend them and bend your hands back at the wrist.
Biceps and upper arms	Clench your hands into fists, bend your arms at the elbows, and flex your biceps.
Shoulders	Shrug them (raise toward your ears).
Forehead	Wrinkle it into a deep frown.
Around the eyes and bridge of the nose	Close your eyes as tightly as you can. (Remove contact lenses before you start the exercise.)
Cheeks and jaws	Smile as widely as you can.
Around the mouth	Press your lips together tightly. (Check your face for tension. You just want to use your lips.)
Back of the neck	Press the back of your head against the floor or chair.
Front of the neck	Touch your chin to your chest. (Try not to create tension in your neck and head.)
Chest	Take a deep breath and hold it for four to ten seconds.
Back	Arch your back up and away from the floor or chair.

MUSCLE GROUP	WHAT TO DO
Stomach	Suck it into a tight knot. (Check your chest and stomach for tension.)
Hips and buttocks	Press your buttocks together tightly.
Thighs	Clench them hard.
Lower legs	Point your toes toward your face. Then point your toes away and curl them downward at the same time. (Check the area from your waist down for tension.)

Always tense and release *very* slowly and *very* smoothly. Some people coordinate their tensing and releasing with their breathing as well. Tense on the inhale, and relax on the exhale. After you get comfortable with each muscle group (and this might take a couple of sessions), link it all together into whole-body progressive muscle relaxation. You choose the order or do a few each time, alternating muscle groups. Maybe start tensing your toes, work all the way to your fingers, and then release the tension the other way around. No matter how you control this, you'll often feel this final sensation: Your last breath is going to come naturally followed by a release of tension that is soon replaced by a gentle wave of muscle relaxation. Allow your muscles to relax into the floor.

RESPONSE STRATEGY #4: ACT IT OUT
Do It to Feel It

What It Is

Research shows it is possible to reduce the intensity of your stress responses by acting as if you are relaxed. We use the word "acting" to describe a process by which a person elicits a true emotion in order to achieve a particular physiological response. It's likely a conditioned response whereby certain body language or words trigger the corresponding emotion.

How does this work? The signals transmitted to the "acting" person's brain are very similar to those that would be transmitted if that person were truly experiencing the same emotion in response to something occurring within his environment. The emotion this person elicits through acting is a true emotion.

The key is this: Actions and thoughts you choose can change the emotions you experience. You do it first. Then you feel it. This change of emotion changes your perceptions, and those changes in perception change how your body responds to the stressors. It's easy to observe such emotional alternation within ourselves.

First, put a deep frown on your face and count to ten. Now observe how you feel, both physically and mentally. Since frowning is the behavioral correlate of frustration, the muscle signals transmitted to the brain elicit the same type of frustration that years of experience have taught the body to associate with it.

Next, form your facial muscles into a smile. Again, count to ten and observe the changes you experience in both your mind and body. Ever since you first smiled back at your mother, you have associated smiling with happiness and comfort. Through conditioning, the smile can elicit positive emotions in the same way a frown will do the opposite.

As you practice this recovery strategy, you will train your brain to follow your thoughts and body's actions. Yes, if you think and act relaxed, it will happen.

Why It Works for You

Just making a choice to do this strategy is good for you. You have taken control, even in a small way, in the face of distress. That willful decision to act, by itself may be enough to help you turn the corner. In turn, these emotions will likely trigger a chain reaction of physiological events that will make a more desired outcome a reality.

The Science Behind It

This recovery strategy is supported with research. Nick carried out an experiment to determine if acting could impact the immune system. The study came about as a result of observations made of a person who had been diagnosed with what is commonly known as multiple personality disorder and which mental health professionals label as dissociative identity disorder. This is a rare and sometimes controversial diagnosis whereby several distinct personalities can be exhibited at different times with each residing in the same body.

Nick designed an experiment during which a small amount of blood was drawn before and after certain preselected personalities were elicited in a thirty-three-year-old female who could control her personas, or whose personas could be elicited by her psychiatrist.

He then selected the persona likely to be associated with changes in the immune system. For example, one of her personas experienced allergies, while another exhibited mild depression. Yet a third upbeat and optimistic personality emerged when her body became ill. These switches between personas caused measurable changes in the number and activity of her white blood cells consistent with those hypothesized to be associated with the respective mood changes.

Despite having only a single subject and therefore limited options for interpretation, this was still a remarkable observation that prompted another study. Were the changes in her body associated with the underlying pathology that manifested itself in the disorder, or would it be possible for someone simply to act in different ways and experience similar changes?

To test this, two professional actors, a male and

a female, were selected to play contrasting roles. In one play both actors assumed the role of a depressed person. After a brief intermission, a second thirty-minute play was performed, and the same actors played upbeat, humorous roles. The two plays were presented nightly for several days before different live audiences.

Before and after each of the performances, the actors' heart rates were recorded using portable heart rate monitors, and blood samples were collected for the assessment of their immune systems. Nick was amazed to observe that simply acting depressed was correlated with impaired immunity.

The results represented powerful evidence that the mind can impact the immune system. Bill Moyers used this research to open the Emmy Award–winning PBS program *Healing and the Mind*. Nick later learned anecdotal evidence that demonstrated how acting can impact one's mental and physical well-being. He had been asked to present a series of lectures onboard the luxury liner *Queen Elizabeth II* during a transatlantic voyage. Shirley Jones, the Oscar-winning actress and television star, was also speaking. Nick happened to ask her if she had ever played a role that impacted her health. She answered "Yes!" without hesitation, describing how depressed and physically ill she felt after her role in *Yesterday's Child*, where she played a mother whose three-year-old daughter was kidnapped without a trace.

How to Do It

The "act it out" Response Strategy causes your body's chemistry to follow your mind and emotions. When distress comes, you can:

- ⊙ Intentionally act as if you are relaxed and in control.

- ⊙ Say out loud, "I am not as relaxed as I would like to be."

- ⊙ No matter how you're feeling at the moment, put a smile on your face.

- ⊙ Pick a positive personal expression that you can speak out loud whenever you feel stressed, such as, "Today I choose to believe the best in others."

- ⊙ Move your body to energize it. Motion creates positive emotion. Do a little jig or happy dance.

- ⊙ Stand tall. Good posture produces positive emotions and a positive mental state. Poor posture lends itself to a poor mental and emotional state.

- ⊙ Remind yourself that problems are not permanent. Problems can help us grow. Keep the big picture in mind rather than only focusing on the problem at hand. This too shall pass.

By acting positive, you'll replace the distressing emotions of fear and uncertainty with those of control and success.

RESPONSE STRATEGY #5: PAUSE IT

Buying Time for Better Choices

What It Is

When stressors bombard you, sometimes the best option is to do nothing. When a stressor triggers your stress response, your brain will tell you it's time for fight or flight.

- ⊙ Maybe your former spouse phones and tells you everything is your fault.

- ⊙ Maybe your baby threw up on your expensive new dress just as you were leaving for a party.

- ⊙ Maybe finances are very tight, you just opened a bill from your cell phone company, and it's twice what you expected.

- ⊙ Maybe your boss just chewed you out and you're ready to give him a piece of your mind.

- ⊙ Maybe you were exposed to a disease that caused you to be isolated alone or with the same group of people for too long, and tensions started to rise.

Are these good times to react? Probably not. Sometimes, when you're *not* in a truly threatening situation, reactions can make things much worse. Perhaps the better option is to press your pause button, back away from the trigger mentally and/ or physically, and give yourself some time to recover before you do anything.

Yes, sometimes doing nothing is the best choice, but only if you regard your nonresponse as one of several options. Don't do "nothing" out of despair and a feeling of helplessness. You are still in control; you are still the one making choices.

The Science Behind It

Depending upon how much pressure you're facing, your brain is going to direct you to respond in one of three basic ways: withdrawal, action, and higher processing.

Withdrawal. You may well have experienced withdrawal after feeling overwhelmed. You don't know where to turn or what to do, so you shut down and do nothing. This may not be a bad thing. After all, if you aren't sure what action to take, doing nothing may well prevent you from digging an even deeper, stress-filled hole. But shutting down is just as likely to keep you from taking a potentially life-saving action. It all depends. Unicellular animals, such as amoebas, have no choice. When threatened with danger, their only option is to shut down and conserve energy, hoping they survive the threat. For us, inaction may be manifested in the extreme as severe depression. On the other end of the spectrum, it might be displayed in the form of procrastination.

Action. An alligator doesn't lie there and take it when approached by a threat. The reptile can either fight or flee. Realize that fighting does not mean arming yourself with an arsenal of weapons and eliminating the threat. It more often is displayed as taking active steps to resolve the issue instead of walking away. As was true with shutting down, it's not the response that's good or bad; it's the appropriateness of the response within a particular environment that determines its value.

Higher Processing. Instead of reacting without thinking, humans have brains with well-developed prefrontal lobes. This enables us to associate future rewards and punishments with the various options we might be contemplating. We assess the situation, tap into memory centers, reflect upon what has happened in the past, then project into the future in an attempt to predict the consequences of the choice we make. In other words, we draw upon multiple brain regions, which is why it's referred to as higher processing.

The different layers of the brain play a part in this strategy. The inner part of the brain will want to freeze and seize. The reptilian brain will want to run for the swamp or bite somebody's head off. Pressing the pause button gives you a chance to engage with the highly developed outer reaches of the human brain, catch your breath (literally and figuratively), take control of your thoughts, and then choose how you will respond. In one instance, a lady in St. Petersburg, Florida, should have waited a minute to respond. Instead, she fired a .38-caliber revolver at a policeman. "Woman Fires at Cop, Virus Stress Is Cited" headlined the story in the Tampa Bay Times article describing how "she was anxious about COVID-19."[38]

How to Do It

Pressing the pause button is as simple as removing yourself physically or mentally from the stressor. But just because this recovery strategy is simple doesn't mean it will be easy, because those inner layers of your brain are going to be telling you to do something else. Doing nothing can be difficult sometimes. Thinking through your plans ahead of time is a good idea so you can engage your outer brain when your stress response is being triggered.

- When your former spouse unleashes on you, tell him or her you need to think about it for a moment and you will call them back. Then hang up.

- When the baby throws up on your brand-new expensive dress just as you're leaving for a party, pause for a moment and take a deep breath. Think about it. The baby didn't mean any harm, and a trip to the dry cleaner should make the dress just like new.

⊙ If the bill from the cell phone company shocks you and your heart starts beating furiously, push back from the desk. Do nothing. Look around. You're still alive, aren't you? Use your outer brain to tell the rest of your brain that you're not in immediate danger. In time, return to the desk and start thinking about options. You've got options.

⊙ When the boss takes his or her frustrations out on you, buy yourself some time and space. Visiting the restroom in the middle of a board meeting is better than losing your temper unnecessarily.

During those times when you automatically shut down, try to discern what is causing you to freeze. This gives you a choice. You can say, "You know what, *that* ticked me off. And because of *that*, I'm going to respond by *this* decision and action." This shifts your thinking into your outer brain and your frontal cortex where you can start to organize the problem, think about it, and choose what to do about it.

How long do you pause? Take as long as you need. A few seconds might be all you need. A few minutes can make a huge difference, but you might need hours, days, or longer. But please be aware that if you are taking time to shut down as a Response Strategy, that's a good thing. But if you're shutting down because your primitive brain has taken over and you're frozen because you're overwhelmed, that's a problem. And the problem is only going to compound if you become less effective at work or start not fulfilling your role in your family, or if the issue descends into depression. You can end up in a downward spiral that can be almost impossible to stop. So when it gets really rough out there, press the pause button and buy yourself time to make better choices. You'll be glad you did.

RESPONSE STRATEGY #6: ROCK IT
Swaying Away the Stressors

What It Is

Just about all mothers learn from experience or instruction that one of the surest ways to calm an infant is to rock them gently. When I (Dick) could not sleep as a young child, my mother would pick me up and gently rock me until I dozed off into a deep slumber. And how many times after slamming your finger in a doorjamb have you grabbed your hand and then rocked back and forth as you lament your circumstances? Even some autistic children who seem overwhelmed with sensory information appear to experience solace when they engage in a repetitive rocking motion.

Think about situations where you have found yourself rocking in the face of adversity or have observed others doing it. When you do, you'll be surprised at all the ways this Response Strategy is utilized. After the World Trade Towers were targeted on 9-11, many airports installed rockers to calm nervous passengers. Several years ago, while lecturing in

Boston, a member of the audience told me (Nick) about a local hospice group that was using suspended beds capable of being rocked for their patients. It was found to be a highly effective way to help people cope during the final phase of the life cycle. When it comes to stress response triggers, rocking is a natural way to be reactive. We are going to use this Response Strategy to be proactive.

Why It Works for You

Research has shown that moving your head through about the same range of motion experienced in a rocking chair has a highly reproducible calming effect. When you rock and your head moves slightly downward, there's enough additional pressure to activate a calming circuit. Many people find that a neck massage can accomplish the same result. A back-and-forth motion with a slight lowering of the head could have the same calming effect.

The Science Behind It

The forward and slightly downward movement of your head activates the parasympathetic nervous system, which can help bring about a calming effect. The stress response is characterized by the sympathetic nervous system, increasing heart rate and elevating blood pressure. Both these actions speed the delivery of oxygen and energy substrates to where they're needed. If blood pressure rises too much, however, it's detected by sensors located in the walls of the major vessels carrying blood to the brain. They are called the carotid arteries that course within your neck before entering the brain through the base of the skull. When even slightly elevated blood pressure stimulates these baroreceptors, they signal the parasympathetic control centers in the brain stem to reduce the pressure. This is done by slowing the heart rate and dilating blood vessels—the same changes that occur when you relax.

How to Do It

Just get in the motion for a while. It's not *rocket* science; it's *rocking* science.

- The classic rocking chair works great.

- Porch swings also create the desired motion.

- You can also create this motion while sitting in an office chair or standing up.

Hammocks and the gentle sway of a boat will work as well, but probably for other reasons. Why not add rocking to your Stretch It and Pause It Strategies? This really works. Whether on a porch swing with Grandma or swaying to the music in your living room, you'll be swaying away your stressors.

RESPONSE STRATEGY #7: LAUGH IT UP

Laughter is Still the Best Medicine

What It Is

It's commonly said, "Laughter is the best medicine." Laughing at our stressors and ourselves is a powerful stress management strategy. When your stress response is being triggered, there's nothing like laughter to help you calm down.

Under extreme conditions, some people resort to jokes just to survive. It's referred to as *gallows humor* in hospital and law-enforcement situations. Both of us have seen this. Nick, when teaching stress-management at the FBI National Academy, worked with an agent who had to respond to the Oklahoma City bombing. His job was to identify the explosives as quickly as possible. They flew him out within an hour of the explosion. He was ordered to focus on identifying the explosives so they could begin chasing the murderer... and ignore the body parts and bleeding adults and children that were wounded and dying. In the midst of the overwhelming carnage, he started telling horrible dead baby jokes to the first responders. It was absolutely appalling and inappropriate. But when Nick spoke to him afterward, he said, "I had to do that. I've got children the ages of the kids I was working around. The only way I could keep myself focused was by telling these detestable jokes to counter the fear and anger that were about to overwhelm me." Gallows humor allowed him to take a little control in the midst of the horrific chaos. He couldn't control the fear or the anger or the sadness he was experiencing, but telling the jokes was a way he could create a diversion and at the same time have a measure of control over the situation.

In hospital settings, Dick has seen both staff and patients use gallows humor to capture some control in the midst of the worst situations. Frequently, surgeons tell jokes or funny stories while doing the most intricate of surgeries. In one instance, a patient had been reduced to little more than a skeleton because of his cancer. He would come out of his room and flex like a body builder while doing Arnold Schwarzenegger impersonations. Everyone cracked up. He smiled. It sounds macabre, but it worked to reduce stress from the direness of the situation.

Why It Works for You

Appropriate laughter can diffuse a stressful argument. It can release physical tension due to an illness. It can change your mindset and break cycles of depression and anxiety. Humor is the result of highly complex mental processes, and laughter can be triggered by all sorts of things. We all want to sit back and enjoy life and even have a good laugh. Your ability to bring humor into a situation will result in your being a fun person to be around. Of course, this requires a high degree of self-confidence. You have to be able to see life from different points of view. Humor is not simply telling a joke; it is the ability to see what is obvious in a new light that helps us not to take everything so seriously. The goal here, of course, is not to laugh at people, but to find in life something to laugh at. We can get so caught up in our circumstances that the intensity and sharp focus can prevent us from taking a step back and viewing the situation from a different perspective. Humor offers that opportunity. In fact, the best humor is about the everyday minutiae of life seen from a different vantage point.

The Science Behind It

A good laugh stimulates physical changes in your body. Laughter can:

- ⊙ Increase oxygen intake, which benefits your heart, muscles, and all major organs

- ⊙ Increase endorphins, the feel-good chemicals in your body that are produced naturally

- ⊙ Aid in muscle relaxation somewhat like progressive muscle relaxation by first increasing stress and then decreasing it throughout your body

- ⊙ Reduce pain by assisting your body in producing its own painkillers

- ⊙ Improve your mood, thereby making depression, a contributor to chronic illness, less likely. In fact, there is evidence your immune system can benefit significantly from laughter. Negative thoughts can give rise to chemical reactions with the potential of decreasing your immunity while positive thoughts can reverse these same chemical reactions.

How to Do It

Nothing cuts stress quite like laughter. Find funny things that will make *you* laugh. Some ideas we suggest:

- ⊙ Watch old comedy movies.

- ⊙ Read or tell jokes—not the off-color ones that are overtly suggestive and can be offensive, but good old-fashioned humor.

- ⊙ *Far Side* cartoons are great. Classic *Calvin and Hobbes*? The best!

- ⊙ Thanks to the internet, a good belly laugh is only a click away. Take your pick from a wide variety of options.

- ⊙ Search "stress and humor" and see what pops up.

- ⊙ Go to a comedy club and enjoy an evening out with the added benefit of some good laughter.

Go ahead and give it a try. Turn up the corners of your mouth and give a laugh, even if it feels a little forced. Once you've had a laugh, consider how you're feeling. Are your muscles a little less tense? Did you forget about your stressors for a moment? Do you feel more relaxed and optimistic?

That's laughter, one of the best medicines ever.

Making It Automatic

Well done! You've introduced yourself to the seven main tools in the top tray of your toolbox. Like learning to ride a bike, getting comfortable with Response Strategies is going to take some conscious effort at first—you'll be putting your brain to good work. The more you practice, the more you will hardwire these new strategies into the inner layers of your brain. They will become habits requiring much less conscious effort.

RESPONSE STRATEGIES REVIEW

1. **Breathe It Out:** Responding to Stressors One Breath at a Time

2. **Stretch It:** Flexing to Avoid Snapping

3. **Let It Go:** Tensing Up to Wind Down

4. **Act It Out:** Do It to Feel It

5. **Pause It:** Buying Time for Better Choices

6. **Rock It:** Swaying Away the Stressors

7. **Laugh It Up:** Laughter Is Still the Best Medicine

The goal is to train your body to trigger your Response Strategies automatically when your heart rate and other stress responses are triggered. How do you do that?

Create a couple of artificial triggers to practice using these responses. The timer on your cell phone is a good place to start. Set it to go off several times a day. When it does, imagine you're in a situation with high stressors and then pick one of the Response Strategies and implement it right there on the spot.

You can also use a heart rate monitor that has an alarm on it. When your heart rate starts to climb for no real reason, use that as a cue to pick one or more of the Response Strategies and do it right there on the spot to bring your heart rate back into an optimal zone.

Congratulations! You're taking control. You're managing your immediate acute stressors. Now you're ready to act and think strategically about your lifestyle.

CHAPTER 5

LIFESTYLE STRATEGIES

Tools to Build Stress Recovery into Your Life

NICK HALL: THE LAST SHALL BE FIRST

I used to be one of the first ones off the beach. I used to push myself to the absolute limit. I've also lost track of the number of times I've gone the wrong direction. Water Tribe events are referred to as "Challenges." However, when two or more competitive individuals find themselves paddling to the same destination, it invariably becomes a race. These epic endurance events on water attract women and men who are driven to compete against others in small human-powered and wind-powered craft, yet we primarily compete against ourselves just to survive and finish.

Important note: Those who try to go fastest often end up last—or don't finish at all.

One time I was paddling my kayak out of Flamingo, the last checkpoint before the finish in Key Largo. It's about 40 miles across through a beautiful, pleasant ecosystem. Most competitors took off around midnight to get ahead. I waited until the sun came up. After I set out, I saw Dirty Little Runner Gal, who had set out hours before me, coming back in. (She got her name from training for marathons in the Arizona desert; she's always covered with sweat and dirt.) "Hey gal, are you okay? Do you need anything?" I figured she'd run out of water or forgot something. She looked at me like "what?" I said, "You're going back?" She had wanted to go fast—and she did maintain very good speed—but half of it was going in exactly the wrong direction, and she didn't even realize it.

I've been there. In the early years, I was always pushing, pushing, pushing, and making an inordinate number of mistakes. Once, in the middle of the night, I took a shortcut and got lost in the mangroves where everything looked the same. I couldn't get a GPS signal, and fog blocked the stars. I lost a lot of time on that shortcut because I ended up getting turned around and, like Dirty Little Runner Gal, arriving back where I had started. Finally, after about six years of pushing to go faster, I got it. I finally caught on about "going slower to go faster." I now do what two very good friends, Paddle Carver and Tyro, do. They're both in their late eighties, yet they regularly beat teams one quarter their age (a classic case of the tortoises against the hares). How? They just do it smart.

When you go slower, you can be more observant, more mindful. Slowing down allows you to take in more information, have a broader perspective, and be able to think so you can predict—and if you can predict, you can plan. This gives you a plan to pace yourself. It gives you the mental capacity to keep *the goal in mind, and you make fewer mistakes and have the physical capacity to go the distance. That's what saves time and makes you faster.*

Now, I'm not the first one off the beach. When the whistle blows and everybody races to the surf, that's when I'll wait and watch to see how the others are doing along the course they chose, and I'll think. THEN I'll launch and follow the course chosen by the sailors making the best time. I'll gather critical information about the conditions and how they impact vessels just like mine at that exact moment. Then, with the additional up-to-date information, I'll predict the best plan for myself.

Yes, in a Water Tribe Challenge, you sometimes need to go slower to go faster.

IN THE RACE OF LIFE

You can probably see where we are going with this. We are in this challenge called life for the long haul. There will be times of intense pressure when we need to sprint and deal with acute stressors. That's when the seven Response Strategies from chapter 4 are most helpful. That's when we might truly have to fight or flee for our physical survival. But life is usually much more like a marathon than a sprint, isn't it?

The top tray of your Stressor-Management Toolbox, the Recovery Strategies, helps you *repair* and *survive*. But deeper in the box we find the tools we need to design and build a better life. Lifestyle Strategies are what we need to *endure* and *thrive*.

When you learn to use both Recovery Strategies and Lifestyle Strategies, you have the ultimate win-win scenario for stress management. And, on top of that, you're going to enjoy the process by having a lot of fun along the way.

The following seven Lifestyle Strategies accomplish two objectives. They (1) reduce distress and (2) enlarge the shape of your Optimal Zone. This is accomplished by minimizing inappropriate responses to some stressors while increasing your capacity to deal with others in a positive way. These tools are innovative, life-altering, and life-enhancing approaches to stress management—scientifically based strategies that truly make a difference. As in the last chapter on Recovery Strategies, chapter 5 is segmented into seven compact subchapters that give you seven powerful tools for managing stress to your advantage over the long haul.

1. **Think About It:** Engaging Your Outer Brain for the Better

2. **Sense It:** Creating Environmental Eustress

3. **Reduce It:** Cutting Stressors Off at the Source

4. **Forgive It:** Finding Freedom from the Past

5. **Move It:** Exercise Always Wins the Day

6. **Eat It Up:** Ingesting the Good Stuff

7. **Give It a Rest:** Taking Intentional Breaks for Ultimate Performance

Imagine you're on the beach with Nick. The whistle blows and everyone starts running for the waves. You can follow the crowd if you wish; it will be just one more day in the dog-eat-dog rat race. Or you can join him on the beach for a little longer. To talk. To watch. To think. To predict. THEN you can plan a wise route into a better future. We are going to use Lifestyle Strategies to slow things down so you can make better choices about how to respond to the stressors in your life.

LIFESTYLE STRATEGY #1: THINK ABOUT IT

Engaging Your Outer Brain for the Better

Why It Works

If you're willing to slow down and become aware of your thoughts in an introspective way, you have taken a huge first step toward managing your stressors. Why? It's important to understand that feeling follows thought. You can't have a feeling without some thought that triggers that feeling. *The complexity is that the thought may be conscious or unconscious. But the thought is there. The good news is you can change your thoughts. It's just like watching TV. If you don't like the channel you are currently on, you can get the remote and change it. With some practice, you can do the same with your thoughts.*

You *can* change what you are thinking about. Just remember, you can't do it by telling yourself to stop thinking about something. Then you are thinking about it more! Rather, think about something else, focus on that, and your thoughts will change. Here's the good news: When you change your thoughts, your perceptions can be changed, and those changed perceptions will change the way your stress responses are triggered, which will change the way you feel.

The Science Behind It

Your brain—that cluster of billions of neurons inside your head—is absolutely astounding. It's impossible to overestimate the power of the human brain, so engaging your brain in your stress management strategy is vital. One of the amazing features of the outer human brain, the cortex, is its capacity for self-awareness, introspection, and decision-making. This can override the more primitive inner layers of the brain. Think about this! *You have the capacity to be aware of your thoughts. You have the capacity to change your thoughts.* Psychologists call this "metacognition." Metacognition is one of the abilities that appears to separate humans from other life forms. We can choose to engage in this higher level of thought. If we don't, we're going to be reacting to outside triggers without any rational thought.

The amazing design of the outer brain—the prefrontal cortex in particular—gives you the capacity to override the more primitive systems deeper within the brain. Anytime you "think about it" you are engaging higher levels of mental processing, which can lead to more informed perceptions, which can lead to healthier actions and reactions.

How to Do It

We suggest four fresh ways to Think About It:

1. Watch Your Words

2. Reframe

3. Visualize

4. Worry Space

Let's unpack them one by one.

Watch Your Words

When we tell people "I have a lot of work to do," or if we keep saying, "I'm so busy I can't keep up," we are confirming these statements as facts to ourselves. The more we tell ourselves "There's no way I'll be able to succeed" at an important project, the more we convince ourselves that we will fail.

How you talk does affect your feelings. Studies have shown that people who tell themselves they are tired actually feel more tired than those who don't, regardless of the amount of sleep they've had or how much they have exercised recently. If we say, "I'm busy all the time," we attract the frantic feeling of being overwhelmed. How you respond sets your mind toward something positive or negative. And negative thoughts increase our stress.

Our bodies react to what our minds are saying whether it's positive or negative. Studies indicate that positive repetitive thoughts enable recovery from anxiety, which means editing your words is a great idea.

Start first by paying attention to the words you're using to describe your day. When someone asks you how things are going, what do you typically say? If you notice you're answering with anxiety-inducing statements, change them. Learn to train your brain to think positively. This will keep you off the path of constant worry. Here are some helpful ways to do this:

- Send notes of gratitude each day expressing something you appreciate about another person. Send a text, write a note, or give a quick shout-out on social media. You might make their day, and you will certainly improve yours.

- Record one positive experience each day. We are big fans of journals. Writing things down forces your brain to process the thought differently and lock it into your memory.

- Say to yourself each day, "I am thankful that I'm not _____" (fill in the blank) and meditate once a day on blessings you are thankful for.

- Replace negative thinking habits with one or more positive habits. Maybe the endless stream of talk radio raises your heart rate. Listen to some good music or a positive podcast instead. Does the complaining in the employee lounge get you riled up? Take your lunch somewhere sunny—literally and figuratively.

⊙ Replace negative sentences with a positive approach. For example, say, "I'm glad I have_____" instead of "I wish I had_____."

At first this won't feel genuine because feelings *follow* thoughts. Using positive words helps break a cycle of negative thoughts and feelings. Negative thoughts cause negative feelings, which cause more negative thoughts. Using your outer brain, you override the feelings stimulated by the inner layers of your brain. By taking control of the thoughts in your outer brain, the feelings will start to fall into line, and genuine feelings will follow. People who use these strategies improve their happiness and reduce their anxieties—and you can too.

Reframing

Reframing changes your perception of a situation. You basically take the same facts and choose to see them differently, from a healthier point of view. For example, when Dick was fired from his job, he viewed his boss as someone who didn't care and was glad to get rid of him. While this is how it felt to Dick, in fact this was not true. His boss was given a mandate by the board to reduce expenses, and the consultants saw Dick's position as one that could be eliminated when times were tough. He chose this option as a way of meeting corporate goals. No doubt this was a difficult decision for him. This thought process doesn't change reality, but it does reframe how Dick sees the situation today, and as a result, thinking about this past situation is less upsetting and stressful for him. Reframing can help you recover from stress more quickly too, and it's an important strategy to prevent distress from kicking in.

Life rarely goes the way you want it to. Still, the stressors don't have to be overwhelming. They can be reframed.

- ☉ Change your perception by reframing the stressor in light of how you've successfully negotiated adversity in the past.

- ☉ Compare your situation using the "things could be worse" approach.

- ☉ Ask others how they view a situation to get a fresh perspective.

Reframing will change the picture you see for the better. As a Lifestyle Strategy, reframing can significantly increase your well-being.

Visualization

In stressful situations, Dick often tells his racers, "Picture it! Don't think it!" What does he mean by this? It's often better to create a mental image in your mind rather than use logic to think through complicated and stressful issues. Thinking is a sequential process; you must get everything to line up for your reasoning to make sense. For example, if a racer is trying to figure out the best way to get through a corner, he must think, *When and where do I hit the brakes while downshifting? How much throttle do I add at the apex? What should my motor speed be when I come out of the corner?* There are dozens of variables to consider. The more a racer thinks about all those variables, the more they slow him down because thinking about them takes time. But if the racer can create a picture or short movie in their mind, they can experience it all at one time. They can see the moisture on the track. They can feel the motorcycle underneath them. They can see themselves doing exactly what they need to do to succeed.

You can do the same thing to prepare yourself for the stressful situations you face every day. The left side of the human brain is responsible for sequential, logical thinking. The right side of the brain is more holistic, colorful, and visual. Looking at a picture can give you more information and insight than mentally talking yourself through a situation. Much more can happen in a picture than in a logical progression.

Images drive the brain. These mental pictures drive our thinking. There are two ways to get the images in your mind: (1) you can watch them live as they're coming in, or (2) you can create your own images like a movie in your brain.

You don't have to respond to what your senses are telling you about the circumstances around you. You *can* create your own images in your mind. Visualized images are transduced into electrochemical signals in your brain just as a real image would be. Those images are going to be filtered through your beliefs, your past experiences, and your values. The images can help you make decisions on what to approach or avoid and also help you control your emotions and stress response.

World-class athletes spend significant time imagining what they intend to do; they mentally rehearse just as they physically practice. If you're trying to learn a new sport, such as whitewater rafting, you can precondition yourself by watching YouTube videos of other whitewater rafters.

When a person envisions doing an activity, the connections are quicker. So, by mentally rehearsing, you're enabling the depolarization of one neuron to transmit that message to the next one faster.

People have employed this strategy for a long time. Now, through increased understanding of neurology, we know why it works. And it works in stress management, too.

How do we create these images?

- ⊙ Recall your favorite memories. Remember your favorite beach, the mountains, your grandmother's kitchen. Recall and visualize one of the successes you had in a similar situation. Think of that time when everything was clicking and all your resources came together just right.

- ⊙ Imagine your best outcome. Take some time to visualize what healthy relationships would look like, what it would feel like to achieve the important goal at work. Contemplate what it would look like to be relaxed and in control.

- ⊙ Rehearse these images in your mind. Repeatedly practice this type of thinking to help the pictures become automated and natural.

- ⊙ Now imagine yourself embracing these visualizations when stressors come your way.

We can all use this strategy for stress management. By closing our eyes, putting ourselves in a better place, and contemplating better outcomes, the body responds by lowering or reversing the stress response.

Worry Space

We are big fans of setting aside a time and place to do your stressing. Why? Classical conditioning can impact your life for both good or bad in ways you may not expect. For example, if you worry while lying in bed or sitting in your favorite chair, the worry cycle can become associated with that piece of furniture. The next time you lie down on the pillow, you resume worrying where you left off the night before. The same goes for your favorite chair. Therefore, it's important to choose a place that you can reserve for the *exclusive* purpose of worrying. Four results will happen when you establish a "worry spot" and go there on a regular basis.

First, you'll be able to focus on the problem, ponder the options, and work toward a solution—all without interfering with other, more important tasks.

Second, you'll get unscheduled worrying out of your routine. Your brain is smart, and it knows that if you have a time and place to worry in the schedule, it won't have to keep reminding you again and again about the problem.

Third, if you go to your spot repeatedly, soon you'll get sick and tired of your worrisome thoughts, and they may even go away because of "habituation." Imagine eating your favorite meal every day or repeatedly watching the same movie. Eventually even the smell of the food or thinking about the movie will become unpleasant. If you keep going to a certain spot to worry, it's possible you'll be motivated to quit worrying just so you don't have to do it anymore.

Fourth, you give your unconscious mind room to come up with a solution when you are *not* in your worry space. How many times have you struggled to remember a name or number only to find the answer eluding you? Yet when you let the problem go and do something else, the answer comes to mind. Not only can problems in your life be solved consciously, they can also be solved unconsciously. When your conscious efforts to solve problems in your worry spot are not working, let your unconscious work on them. Rather than worrying about the answer, tell yourself that with time the answer will come to you. This conscious confidence will fuel your unconscious brain to succeed.

How can you create your worry space? Here are some ideas:

⊙ Pick a regular place. You may want to choose somewhere uncomfortable. Maybe the dumpster behind your office building. Or an uncomfortable chair in the corner of your garage.

⊙ Pick a consistent time. Maybe take five or ten minutes over your lunch break. Does it make sense to do it in the morning after stressful thoughts may have accumulated during your sleep?

At the very least, stressful thoughts and feelings won't be nearly as disruptive in your worry space as they would be somewhere else. And, significantly, you will have gained control over them in a stress-reducing way.

Never underestimate the power of your outer brain. Always take advantage of the powerful capacity you have for metacognition—the ability to think about your thoughts and control your choices. In your overall stress-management strategy, and in your quest to stay in the performance zone, your willingness and ability to "think about it" is your most important tool. Everything else you do will flow from this one Lifestyle Strategy. So think about *that*!

LIFESTYLE STRATEGY #2: SENSE IT
Creating an Environment of Eustress

Your brain is constantly taking in and assessing massive amounts of sensory information at any given moment. By controlling certain elements in your environment, you can tweak the input your senses are bringing in. This means you can minimize some of the elements that trigger your stress response and optimize the triggers that relax and energize you.

The Science Behind It

Most of the sensory systems course through the brain via elaborate structures and pathways. For example, the senses of hearing and vision wind their way through the sensory apparatus, arriving initially within a structure called the thalamus. From this relay site, the information is transmitted to higher brain centers where it is processed in ways that enable you to interpret and make the appropriate decisions about what is happening in your environment. Eventually the information arrives in the limbic system, the brain's emotional computer. The structures in it help trigger your sympathetic nervous system and subsequent fight-or-flight reactions if warranted.

Through classical conditioning, you have learned to make mental connections between sensory information and positive, healthy inputs. For example, that picture of you and your spouse on your honeymoon connects with all sorts of warm and fuzzy memories. Perhaps the smell of apple pie takes you back to Grandma's house and the good old days. Maybe the sound of the ocean connects in your memory with that time you sat on the beach watching the sunset. Other sensory information can trigger your stress response. If you have a bad experience in your office, re-exposure to a fragrance you associated with the space might evoke the same physiological and psychological outcomes you experienced at the time it happened.

While the thought of a quiet beach may be relaxing for some, other people may smell the ocean breezes and go into immediate panic as they recall having to pull their child free from an undertow that was taking them out to sea. So, again, do what works for you, not necessarily what everyone else is doing.

Placebo effects also come into play. If you *think* something is helping you reduce stress, it's very possible that it will reduce your stress response even though there may be no direct biological connection. The placebo phenomena are very real and should not be dismissed simply because the biological underpinnings can't be easily explained.

As usual, one size doesn't fit all. What kind of environment creates a positive reaction in *you*? What do *you* perceive as stressors in the places you dwell? You'll need to do a little detective work in your own soul to answer these questions for yourself. Here are a few possibilities for creating relaxing environments:

Sights

- ⊙ Put up paintings and pictures of people and things you love.

- ⊙ Use screensavers that make you laugh, smile, and relax.

- ⊙ Adjust your lighting. You can change the color or intensity of the light. Would dimmer lights calm you? Would brighter lights lighten your mood? Some people are bothered by fluorescent bulbs, while others avoid LEDs. Choose the type that is best for you.

⊙ Natural light. Research confirms that sunlight is good for your brain. Open your shades and get outside.

⊙ Reduce distressing sights. Some stressors cause anxiety simply by seeing them. A stack of bills on the counter? A pile of laundry you're not getting to? Put those bills in a drawer and place that laundry in the closet. Do what you can to remove influences you perceive as stressors.

Smells

Your life experiences can be affected by the smells around you. Various applications of aromatherapy exist. Scented oils are sometimes used during massage. Other fragrances are believed to counter various illnesses or induce a state of relaxation. The use of aromatherapy dates back four thousand years to the days of the early Egyptians. While difficult to prove or disprove, aromatherapists claim that the strategic use of scents can affect conditions ranging from arthritis and allergies to anger and depression.

Perhaps some aromatherapists' claims are valid. It's unlikely that a therapy would have endured thousands of years without some basis for it. Don't fall for the ads that tout aromatherapy as a cure-all for what ails you. Still, there's no harm in trying it. Even if it's a placebo, you'll discover which fragrances work for you and help you manage your stress. With a little forethought, you can use aromas and classical conditioning to make connections between what you smell and what you want to think and experience.

Sounds

Your smartphone and a set of earbuds or speakers give you the power to immediately change the feel of your environment. Noise-canceling technologies can even help filter out negative inputs. Some athletes use these technologies to prevent their nerves from taking over before they compete in their given sport. Next time you watch a sporting event, observe athletes before the game and notice how many have on earphones or earbuds.

- ⊙ Consider ambient soundscapes.

- ⊙ Create a playlist of songs you listened to in happy seasons of life.

- ⊙ Create another list of music for inspiration.

- ⊙ Create a playlist of music that soothes you, and use it in times of stress. Instrumental music works best for most people, but pick songs that will calm your nerves, help you unwind, and bring peace. Use this music at home, at work, or on stressful commutes.

One way of putting this strategy into practice is to get out in nature as often as you can. You can experience the sights, sounds, fresh air, sunlight, and exercise all at one time. Dick enjoys getting out in nature very much. It also helps provide him with perspective. Problems that seem large shrink in comparison to the great expanse of the outdoors. So plan an outing into nature. You will be glad you did.

Relationships

The people around you are a significant aspect of your personal environment. Metaphorically speaking, a good relationship is like sunshine, whereas a bad one can follow you around like a dark cloud. The truth is that good friends develop over time. This is necessary because part of the friendship is the history you build together. You can then draw upon and share the memories you develop together as a way of strengthening the bond and reinforcing from the past the good times you will continue to share in the future.

Researchers are now studying the effects of friends and friendships and those attributes that make for good friends. While there have been theoretical writings on this topic, only in recent years have answers to what makes a good friend been empirically researched. This has been the result of researchers' success in defining conceptually and operationally what a good friend is.[39] The bottom line is that relationships are a huge part of your personal environment. Having friends and being a friend are very important.

Why It Works for You

It would be nice if we all had corner offices overlooking the bay and if everyone were a friend. Even though you can't always control your environment, you can control many variables within whatever environment you happen to be: The interior of your car during your daily commute. Your nine-to-five cubicle. Your back porch. Your bedroom. In these places and many more, you can adjust what you see, smell, and hear to control your stressors.

You really can reduce the stressors that trigger your stress response and the sympathetic nervous system. You truly can optimize the inputs that trigger healthy and relaxing responses. Beyond that, taking control of your environment gives you a legitimate sense of control, and that sense of control always helps reduce your stress response.

So give your senses the best of what feels finest to you: Create an environment full of good influences and good people that induce a pleasant atmosphere.

LIFESTYLE STRATEGY #3: REDUCE IT
Cutting Stressors Off at the Source

It is commonly believed that you can slowly heat a pan to boiling with a live frog in it and the frog will make no effort to escape. This is accomplished by raising the temperature a little at a time so the frog doesn't realize it is cooking. Regardless of whether this is true (we have no desire to conduct the experiment), the analogy is valid. Many of us get into situations that seem normal only to have them slowly, over time, erode the quality of our lives. And yet we don't have the common sense to jump out.

What It Is

The Reduce It Lifestyle Strategy for stress management sounds simple: You cut stressors off at the source so they can no longer trigger your stress responses. Sometimes the most obvious action for us to do is to remove the stressors in our lives or, if the stressors can't be changed, to remove ourselves from the stressors. This sounds easy, but doing it can be difficult. Often, we feel locked into a job, relationship, or an environment we can't seem to get out of. More often than not, however, we can make choices, take different routes, and implement adjustments.

What triggers your stress response?

⊙   Is it certain people?

⊙   Does it hit at certain times of the day or night?

⊙   Is it caused by something in your environment?

⊙   What are you doing when this happens? Are you reading the news, watching television, or scrolling through social media sites?

⊙   What are your thought patterns when your stress response gets triggered?

Asking these kinds of questions can help identify triggers that set off your stress response. Establishing an internal anxiety gauge using a scale of 1–10 is also helpful, with 1 being the lowest amount of anxiety you experience and 10 the highest. Using this gauge, you will be able to notice patterns, such as spiking up to 8 when you meet with your supervisor or plunging down to 2 when you hear your favorite song. Over time this exercise will help you recognize your anxiety triggers. Once you've identified some of your triggers, you can then decide if approaching them differently can reduce any of your distress.

Sometimes discovering your triggers and finding alternatives requires some detective work. Dick is currently coaching a nurse who leads a team of other nurses in an intensive care unit. She has done so successfully for years. But now she's being labeled as "failing" by her superiors. The stressors seem to keep piling up on her. She's in her late fifties, and her fears of losing her job are real. "What am I going to do?" she asked him. "I can't go back to floor nursing because I'm getting old, a little bit arthritic, and I can't stand on my feet all that time. I just can't do it. Who else is going to hire me at my age? I feel trapped, I'm getting overwhelmed, and the truth is I just don't know where to begin. So I go into my office and close the door. I don't know what to do."

Dick put a heart rate monitor on her. Sure enough, when she went to work, her heart rate escalated to 120. He started by training her in some of the seven Stress Response Strategies. "You have to start by managing what you can control," Dick told her. She began to implement several of these strategies when she felt her stress responses kicking in:

- ⊙ **Breathe It Out:** Responding to Stressors One Breath at a Time

- ⊙ **Stretch It:** Flexing to Avoid Snapping

198 THE STRESS RECOVERY EFFECT

- ⊙ **Let It Go:** Tensing Up to Wind Down

- ⊙ **Act It Out:** Do It to Feel It

- ⊙ **Pause It:** Buying Time for Better Choices

- ⊙ **Rock It:** Swaying Away the Stressors

These strategies helped, but the sources of her stress response triggers were still there. It was a constant battle. The big picture: Upper management is demanding more from her team with fewer resources. The team is getting overwhelmed and burned out. Employee turnover is high. Those who stay are ready to quit. Many are missing work more and more.

By breaking this massive stressor down into more manageable bites, she is finding solutions that reduce the triggers. For example, they found a new way to manage the incessant stream of urgent emails that bombard her throughout the day. They created a new way to distribute work among the team, resulting in fewer distractions and more focus. They are adjusting the staffing model and communicating more with the emergency room and surgery to ensure they have the right number of staff on hand when patients come to the ICU. These might seem like little changes, but one by one they are minimizing and removing issues that caused her chronic distress. And her heart rate is not spiking as much during the day, so she knows her efforts are working.

Since relationships have a significant impact on stress triggers, you might need to think about putting boundaries between you and a toxic relationship, or even ending the relationship altogether. By managing what you can control in small identifiable steps, you can significantly reduce the distress.

Why It Works for You

The Reduce It Lifestyle Strategy removes or minimizes unwanted stressors at the source—*before* they can trigger your stress response. This is a particularly helpful tool to fix chronic stressors that eat away at you day after day—the repetitive stressors that keep your body on high alert through the fight-or-flight stress response.

How to Do It

First, remind yourself of our two Key Principles:

1. Manage what you can control.

It makes zero sense to try to change things that are out of your control. If your boss's attitude stinks, there's nothing you can really do about that. But you might be able to avoid situations where her attitude triggers your stress response. You might be able to define personal boundaries that somewhat insulate you from her behavior. And remember, you are free to quit.

2. Go slower to go faster.

If reducing stressors was easy, everyone would be doing it. The fact is, the Reduce It principle can be complicated to implement. Rarely is anything in life black and white. Relationships are intertwined and not always easy to discern or navigate. It can be costly to change the status quo. You might have to upset an apple cart or two. To remove or minimize the triggers that cause stress, you will need to slow down and think about this. Maybe *really* think about it to get a handle on the challenges and the best courses of action.

Second, get off the roller coaster for a little while and put your outer brain to good use:

- ⊙ Identify the big problem.

- ⊙ Break the problem down into smaller parts.

- ⊙ Identify what you can control.

- ⊙ Brainstorm all your options.

- ⊙ Create a plan for change.

Let's look at an example. Maybe your commute to work is an ongoing trigger of your stress response. How could you minimize or remove this trigger? Start brainstorming. Some solutions:

- ⊙ Move closer to work.

- ⊙ Find a job closer to your home.

- ⊙ Buy a car that is more comfortable and enjoyable.

- ⊙ Listen to music that is calming for *you*.

- ⊙ Leave a little earlier and take a more relaxing route.

By thinking outside the box, you might surprise yourself with the number of ways you can remove or minimize the triggers to your stress responses. In many situations, you'll find a plan that allows you as a Lifestyle Strategy to "Reduce It" and cut off your stressors at the source.

There are probably many concerns you find distressing

that are outside your control. In those situations, you'll need to incorporate other stress Response Strategies and other Lifestyle Strategies into your stress management plan. But often you only need to be smarter than a frog. Sometimes you just need to jump out of the pot of water. Or maybe at least get out for a while so you can figure out how to turn down the burner.

LIFESTYLE STRATEGY #4: FORGIVE IT
Finding Freedom from the Past

Sometimes in our Stress Recovery Effect seminar we ask people to raise their hand if they think they are an angry person. Usually, one or two in the group will raise their hand; sometimes no one does. Then we ask if they know someone who is an angry person; every hand goes up. That's interesting, isn't it? Angry people must be very popular, because there are so few of them yet everyone seems to know them!

Surprisingly, many people aren't aware of their anger, or at least not to the extent others see their anger. Maybe you have trouble admitting your anger, but can you acknowledge that you've been hurt? Probably. Consider this fact: Most experts consider anger a response to hurt. Our anger can be good in that it musters up the energy to act in the face of our hurt. Anger is the source of energy needed to assert our self and defend our rights. Yet most people are not comfortable with their anger, so they deny its existence. One of the many concerns is that anger mimics stress; anger is both a cause of stress and an indicator of stress's presence.

Why is it that some people seem to explode when something goes wrong, and others simmer much longer? Could it be that we all have a pool of anger built up inside that gets tapped into from time to time? And could that reservoir of anger cause us to be more upset than the current circumstances call for so that we explode at unexpected times? It's important to understand that anger cannot be stored. What is stored are the memories, and every time a memory is recalled, the anger attached to it bubbles back to the surface. And when you have been hurt deeply, it's hard not to think of that event over and over again. But by doing so, you become your own worst enemy. While the other person may have caused you the initial hurt, you alone are keeping it alive today.

You see, anger is not only a result of stress, it's an additional stressor itself that you have to deal with. Anger elevates heart rate and blood pressure just like stress and, if left unchecked, can have the same significant negative consequences upon your health. The real problem is not with the anger itself but rather the retention of your anger. For if anger is not adequately dealt with at the time it occurs, it will come roaring back when you least expect it.

If you are experiencing anger or hurt in some way, pay close attention to this Lifestyle Strategy. You may be among the 20 percent of the general population that has levels of hostility high enough to be dangerous to your health.

The Science Behind It

To help you understand the mechanisms of how anger works, the following cascading events illustrate what can occur in your body when you are upset:

1. Anger is a high-energy emotion associated with stress. Since you are likely to be motivated to engage in some action when angry, you'll need energy in the form of glucose delivered quickly to your muscles and other tissues.

2. Cortisol and adrenaline trigger a rise in blood sugar, while at the same time adrenaline increases blood pressure so the sugar can be rushed to its destination.

3. Cortisol is formed in the adrenal glands from cholesterol, which is made in the liver. That means the cholesterol must be transported in the bloodstream to the adrenals. To facilitate the easy movement of cholesterol through the blood, the cholesterol binds to low-density lipoprotein, or LDL.

4. For short intervals, the body can manage an increase in blood pressure without damaging your health. But if you are angry most of the time and your blood pressure remains elevated for months or perhaps years, eventually the

sides of the blood vessel erode, much like the banks of a river when the current is strong.

5. These hardened blood vessels can trigger inflammation, causing blood-clotting platelets to accumulate along with LDL cholesterol. As a result, plaque begins to form on the lining of your blood vessels.

6. Over time the plaque accumulates, restricting blood flow until eventually the blood stops flowing. If it happens in the coronary arteries it will result in a heart attack. If it happens in the brain, a stroke.[40]

Not a great picture for good heart and vascular health. But the good news is you can do something to reverse it, and the intervention will not require you to pay any out-of-pocket expenses.

What It Is

The old saying "forgive and forget" does not accurately describe what forgiveness is. Forgiveness is not forgetting; rather, forgiveness is remembering in a different way. If your memory of the event changes, your emotional response to that memory will change as well. You may think of forgiving as benefiting the other person or letting them off the hook. But forgiveness is really about you. It brings closure, release, and freedom.

Why It Works for You

When someone has hurt you deeply, you end up thinking about that person a lot, and the repetitive thinking determines your physiologic response. Holding onto that grudge also holds onto that thought and thus keeps you in a stressed response (i.e., high blood pressure). Forgiveness is a way of letting go of that thought because you're reframing it. When you think about it differently, your response is going to be different.

To determine how best to reduce the physiological side effects of anger, Dick conducted original research that demonstrated something astounding: By practicing forgiveness, individuals with high blood pressure may lower their blood pressure and actually reverse the disease of hypertension.

The forgiveness approach has helped thousands of people. It can help you too.

How to Do It

1. Express your anger in an appropriate way.

It is better to express your anger than to repress it. If you repress it, the anger will eat you alive from the inside out. That's not just a figure of speech; the chemicals released because of chronic anger will literally eat away at your stomach, arteries, brain cells, and more.

While rage is the most observable aspect of anger, it's not the most common expression. The most frequent way people deal with their anger is to hold it in. This retained anger can convert to resentment, which often takes on a life of its own.

Feelings from the past can become so real they feel like the old event just happened again, triggering the stress response again and again. Walter Williams summed it up this way: "To carry a grudge is like being stung to death by a single bee."

There are three primary ways of expressing anger:

- ⊙ **Aggressive** – which lashes out toward others. This expression rarely works and often makes things worse.

- ⊙ **Passive** – which tries to bury the anger in hopes it will go away. The problem is that anger is never buried dead; it is buried alive only to come back at another time in inappropriate ways.

- ⊙ **Assertive** – which states the concerns with a desire to resolve the issues and move on.

When expressing anger, be assertive. Stay focused on the issues, but avoid being accusatory. Calm yourself so you can move into a higher level of processing and carefully weigh the options. The following tips may also help:

Write out your thoughts before you speak them. This will help you express your anger assertively rather than aggressively. Taking time to think through your words puts *you* in control rather than your emotions.

Before you express yourself, you may have a hope or a wish for how the other person will respond. Identify what that is, and be prepared to NOT get that response. Why? If you expect that response, you may be disappointed, which can then turn to anger. The purpose of expressing yourself is not necessarily for resolution of the grievance but for you to appropriately let the feelings out so you can move forward.

Remember that you've likely been thinking about the situation for a long time and in a great amount of detail. That is not usually the case for the other person. It may be helpful to provide the context of the situation and/or explain the sequence of events involved.

Be prepared to listen to what the other person has to say. They may fill in some blanks or give you information you didn't know about. With this new information, your initial assessment of the situation may change.

When confronting, use "I" statements to express your point of view rather than "you" statements. "You" statements are more likely to trigger a defensive reaction because they are heard as blame. No one should be able to argue with "I" statements, which simply state how you feel and think about the problem.

Establish consequences and appropriate boundaries where necessary. Behavior has consequences. You want to choose those consequences wisely and not just react to the situation.

2. See the person causing your pain as a mixture of good and bad.

You've heard the expression "love is blind." When someone is in love, all they can see in the other person is their good characteristics. They are "blinded" to the other's faults, only to eventually discover the person was not as good as they thought they were.

The same is true with anger: it is equally blind. When we are angry, we tend to see only the faults of the person we're angry at. However, it's also true that the person has some good qualities as well. That is how your worst enemy can be someone else's best friend. In fact, we are all a mixture of good and bad. How we see each other depends on what characteristics we focus on. We always see what we look for in the other person. Seeing the other as a mixture of good and bad will help reduce the intensity of the anger you're experiencing.

3. Reframe your anger.

Just as stress is amplified by how we interpret the event, so too anger is amplified by how we frame the situation that gave rise to it. Think of it this way: We all frame our life experiences. We choose at some level what to retain in our picture of life and what to leave out. You probably don't think about this much, but your brain does. It needs categories or drawers in which to place memories. And let's be honest, we don't remember everything. We selectively remember events from our past.

This was illustrated when Dick and his sister recently visited the town where they grew up. They shared their memories of the home, the neighborhood, and, most importantly, the friends and family that impacted their childhood so much. But while he and his sister grew up together in the same home and neighborhood, their memories of those experiences were quite different. (Dick's wife was so amused by this that she questioned out loud if they truly grew up in the same home.) How do your childhood memories stack up against those of your siblings? Our guess is they are quite different as well.

This is what we call framing your memories. It is your frame of reference from which you then interpret life around you. If you felt safe as a child, you tend to see life from this perspective. But if your childhood life was scary, you may easily view life as a scary place with uncertainties around every corner.

Once you recognize that life is how you frame it, you can start to reframe your life by adding elements that were left out of your picture or by reducing details that have become dominant in your picture. For example, not every person is abusive, even though some are. So you learn to put the past in perspective. This is not easy work, but it is necessary if you ever hope to escape from your resentment and engage the world in a different way.

4. Take ownership of your feelings.

You've heard the expression "You make me so angry!" When you truly believe that, your thoughts sound like this:

Sound familiar? You are held captive by someone else's past actions when in fact you are choosing to stay there. The other person has moved on and may not even realize you're holding a grudge against them. Why would you place your future happiness in the hands of a person who has demonstrated that they don't care?

On the other hand, when you accept your anger as yours, you can control how you will act on it. In this instance your anger will flow as follows:

- ⊙ I am responsible for how I feel.

- ⊙ You do not determine my feelings.

- ⊙ Therefore, I will choose how I wish to respond and live life my way.

By following this new pathway, you have moved your life from being a victim to being a victor. Don't live a life that someone else has made for you; live the life of your choosing. Take the journey from bitter to better.

5. Forgive to live.

Perhaps the most powerful way to find relief from chronic resentment is to practice forgiveness. Forgiveness begins with the choice to forgive. No one can make you forgive; you must decide for yourself that forgiveness is the best course of action to pursue. You need to know you're doing this for yourself. While most people resist forgiveness because they don't believe the other person deserves it, the truth is that forgiveness benefits the one who forgives far more than it benefits the one forgiven. Forgiveness is necessary for your healing.

However, forgiveness is more than simply saying the words "I forgive." Forgiveness is a process of reframing the events of your past so you don't remain a victim of another person's actions. What they did toward you is their issue; what you choose to do going forward is your life. Rather than reacting to what the other did to you, take charge of your thoughts and actions and determine what you will do to stay in control of your life. It is your life; live it the way you choose.

Forgiveness will also lower the guilt and responsibility you may feel for how the situation came about. Even if you did something wrong, there is nothing to be gained by feeling guilty the rest of your life. You need to forgive yourself as much as you need to forgive others in order to move on.

Forgiveness does not excuse what the other person did, nor does it make their actions right. The opposite is true: You are forgiving because what they did was wrong. You are simply choosing not to be imprisoned by your own constant recollection of the events. Forgiveness is the first step of the journey to letting go of the other person's hold on your life and thoughts and getting back to the life you want to live. Forgiveness places you back in the driver's seat.

Ralph Waldo Emerson once said, "For every minute you are angry, you lose sixty seconds of happiness." You have spent long enough stewing in the bitter juices of resentment and revengeful thoughts. Learn to forgive and live life to its fullest. It's time to let go of the bitterness that has held you back and move forward with the life you were meant to live. Make the decision to no longer give the other person free rent in your head. It's time to smell the roses again and get your life back on track toward what it was meant to be. Forgiveness will get you there.

To learn more about forgiveness and how to apply it to your life, Dick has written a book titled *Forgive to Live*.[41] Like the book you are reading now, *Forgive to Live* was based on research conducted by the author as well as the feedback from thousands of participants who went through the Forgive to Live program. Forgiveness is not easy work, but it's essential work if you ever hope to move beyond the resentment and anger you may be harboring against someone who has harmed you. Remember, the other person may have started the hurt, but you are the one who is keeping it alive.

LIFESTYLE STRATEGY #5: MOVE IT

Exercise Always Wins the Day

Imagine you're waiting in the checkout line of your local grocery store. You glance over at the tabloid headlines and notice that aliens have been discovered on the far side of Venus, So-and-So celebrities are breaking up, and English royalty is misbehaving yet again. In between the captions about miracle diets that have just been discovered, you see another headline that announces to the world:

Amazing Remedy Found! A Single Daily Dose:

- ⊙ Lengthens your lifespan
- ⊙ Decreases heart disease
- ⊙ Improves your social life
- ⊙ Promotes happiness and well-being

- ⊙ Revitalizes your sex life

- ⊙ AND improves your capacity to manage stressors of all kinds.

Another story that's too good to be true, right? Wrong. This one turns out to be scientific fact. What is this amazing remedy? It's exercise.

What It Is

Exercise is intentionally placing stress on the body. Remember in chapter 1, we defined stress as either a pressure or a tension. When you exercise, you are literally stressing the systems in your body by strategically causing tension and pressure in one way or another.

Why It Works for You

The dictionary says exercise is "an activity which requires physical effort, carried out to improve or sustain health and fitness."[42] Exercise also provides a chance for you to get away from the stressors in your normal routine, whether you like to find some solitude like Nick or engage with friends and build networks like Dick.

If you start slowly and build gradually, you can minimize the inevitable discomfort that accompanies the early stages of any new exercise routine. Soon you'll notice that your waistline shrinks, your stamina and strength increase, and you feel a new sense of control, energy, and mental focus that will help you not only survive but even thrive in stressful situations.

The Science Behind It

Exercise causes the body to produce endorphins, which are chemicals in the brain that are natural painkillers and mood enhancers. Endorphins are similar in chemical composition to morphine and codeine and have a similar calming effect on the mind and body—but without the destructive side effects. Your body releases endorphins when you push yourself beyond your stagnant existence, and because they mask the pain of your efforts, you can go even farther than you thought you could. In the end, endorphins give you the wonderful euphoric feeling of relaxation and optimism that accompanies a solid workout.

Exercise revs up your body, just like stress does. The difference is that after you exercise, your heart rate and blood pressure slow down, and your body returns to normal. But with most of the stress you experience, your body revs up and stays revved up. If you exercise when revved up by stress, you may trick your body into a faster physical recovery from that stressor.

Excessive exercise, however, can be detrimental. For example, marathon runners are more prone to upper respiratory infections for two weeks after a race. Anorexics will often use exercise to curb their appetite. Obligate runners can become addicted to endorphins and continue to push themselves despite injury to avoid withdrawal symptoms.

Not too much, not too little. You are always aiming for the Optimal Zone.

How to Do It

1. Do what's fun.

Fun. That's rule number one, first and foremost. If *fun* is the driver behind your exercise, you'll never have to worry about where you end up. Thus, exercise has a doubling effect. Not only do you get the stress-reducing effects of the exercise, but the fun aspect is stress-reducing as well.

Sex is a great stress-reducing exercise for this very reason. Sex also flips a switch that turns off the stress response from the sympathetic nervous system and turns on the parasympathetic nervous system when it's over. This lowers heart rate and respiration afterward. Sex also releases oxytocin, which under the right conditions can induce a sense of belonging and unity.

2. Go aerobic.

When you think "aerobic," think *breathing*. Aerobic exercises can get your heart rate up and work your muscles in ways that deplete them of oxygen, causing you to breathe a lot harder. Aerobic exercises help you build endurance.

Walking, jogging, running, swimming, and biking are great ways to get your body breathing hard.

3. Go anaerobic.

When you think "anaerobic," think *burning*. Anaerobic exercises are intense enough to cause lactic acid to form in your muscles. This type of training builds strength, speed, power, and muscle mass.

Weightlifting, push-ups, sit-ups, pull-ups, hiking steep hills, and running up steps are all great ways to get the burn.

4. Do intervals.

Whether you're going for breathing or the burn, intervals are an important part of maximizing the effects of your exercise for stress management. The principle is simple: Vary the intensity of your efforts over time. In a single workout, you might push yourself into the high-breathing or high-burn stages four or more times, with some resting or coasting in between. In a single week, you might have workouts that are more intense than others, giving your body more time to recover in between. Many athletes even vary the intensity of their workouts week to week and month to month.

In chapter 7 we'll show you a specific interval exercise strategy that trains your body to recover after acute stressful events.

5. Go the distance.

Are the stress-reducing chemicals released by exercise addictive? Honestly, yes. Exercise should come with a notice similar to the one on a pack of cigarettes:

Warning: The Surgeon General of the United States has determined that exercise, if done repeatedly, can become a highly addictive, mood-enhancing, health-improving, and social-

stimulating habit you won't want to break. Exercise will cause you to crave more and more of it, disrupting normal routines in your life, such as sitting on the couch, eating junk food, and binge-watching an endless stream of reruns on TV.

Yes, be warned. When you get hooked on exercise, you never know how far you will go with the habit. Stories abound of people who started innocently by walking around the neighborhood. Then (often due to the peer pressure of newfound friends) they decided to jog a couple blocks. But they wanted more of the "runner's high" and proceeded to run a 5K and even a full marathon.

6. Unwind when done.

When you are done exercising, cool down with the progressive muscle relaxation Response Strategy we showed you in chapter 4. Maybe do the tense and release exercise before taking some of those deep breaths while rocking on the porch swing. NOW take a break. You've earned it.

The bottom line is that exercise is a powerful and versatile tool for stress recovery. It's certainly one of the most important in your entire toolbox of Lifestyle Strategies. Learn to use it well. It will change your life for the better.

 ## LIFESTYLE STRATEGY #6: EAT IT UP
Ingesting the Good Stuff

It was 115 degrees when Nick pedaled his bicycle over the Colorado River into Arizona. Having reached the age of sixty-seven, he had left California earlier in the week with Florida as his destination. He expected to encounter high temperatures on his three-thousand-mile ride. But what he didn't expect was the effect boredom would have on him during the four-week, coast-to-coast ride. Cycling solo, he had no one to talk to during daily rides that required covering an average of one hundred miles in order to get back in time to start his teaching job. He spent most nights camped in abandoned buildings, behind truck stops, or in public parks. There was very little in the way of pleasure to counter the monotony of the barren landscapes of West Texas and during the long climbs up desolate mountain passes.

Those times were stressful in every sense of the word. Nick started craving some form of pleasure and relief. Under stress, with few options for pleasure, he turned to food. It never took him long to locate the baked goods section in a convenience store, where he found his favorite delicacy: a paper-wrapped toasted apple pie. He devoured it. But he didn't stop there. By sunset he had devoured burgers with fries, ice cream, and a box of Fig Newtons. That was between a hearty breakfast and robust dinner at whatever restaurant was likely to deliver fast service with generous portions of calorie-laden foods.

Aware of the need for essential nutrients, he would also grab a couple of bananas, apples, and peaches. He made it a point to have at least one large salad per day whenever possible. Under normal circumstances, the types of foods he was eating would have wreaked havoc on his cardiovascular system. But like endurance athletes competing in other types of events, the extra demands placed on his body had to be met.

Few people would start their day with three fried-egg sandwiches, each adorned with cheese, lettuce, tomatoes, and fried onions followed by a large omelet, a helping of grits, French toast, chocolate chip pancakes, and two cups of coffee. But that's what Michael Phelps, the most decorated athlete in the history of the Olympics, ate while training for the 2008 Beijing games.[43] It would be followed by hours in the pool during which he likely burned off many of the estimated three thousand calories he consumed at each meal. For Phelps, food was fuel, and without the extra calories his muscles would have been unable to keep up with the demands being placed upon them.

In Nick's case, everything was working the way it was supposed to. He was stressing his body through cycling and burning the calories he took in. But what if he had been experiencing stress without the exercise? The same stress-induced brain chemicals emotionally broadcasting their "feed me" signal would still be present. However, instead of being burned off with each turn of the pedals, they would have become packaged as fat. That's what often happens with stressed-out people. And maybe it's happened to you. Nutritionists are well aware of this food-mood connection. We often eat not because we are hungry but because we are stressed. Cortisol, the primary stress hormone, makes pleasurable activities more intense. Scientists at the Rockefeller Institute think that stress makes us want more pleasant-tasting comfort foods[44]

Have you ever had to struggle to make ends meet, or lived in a bad relationship? Have you ever felt overworked at a job, or struggled with a painful illness? In those difficult

220 | THE STRESS RECOVERY EFFECT

times, you might notice it's easy to turn to comfort foods as a source of pleasure or escape—especially when other options for pleasure are not available. The body may start craving rich foods because it believes there is a need for additional calories to fuel the fight-or-flight response. In the short run, the strategy can be amazingly effective. But in the long run, weight gain can occur along with associated conditions like cardiovascular disease, inflammation, and diabetes. Those, in turn, will become a secondary source of stress. Still, food is often our go-to when facing distress of all kinds. Consider the worst day you've had in the last couple of weeks. What did you eat? Most likely it was high-carbohydrate meals. Stress drives down brain levels of serotonin, which triggers a craving for carbohydrates.[45]

There are different types of carbohydrates, some with simple structures and others more complex. Fiber is also a part of this category of macronutrient. However, while important, fiber does not contribute significant energy to the human diet. Carbohydrates are comprised of sugar molecules. The simple ones will result in elevated blood sugar soon after digestion, while the more complex ones raise the blood sugar more slowly for sustained energy. Regardless, both provide the energy that cells need to perform their specialized functions. The stress hormone cortisol functions to release additional glucose from storage so a person has sufficient energy if needed. During times of stress, when chemicals in the brain trigger a craving for carbohydrates, we need to fuel everything from the brain to the immune system.

In the end, overeating can be both a symptom and a

cause of stressors. Knowing how this happens will make it easier to take control and make better choices that will give you a healthier body, mind, and spirit. By ingesting healthy foods at the right time, you can even help minimize and combat the stressors you face every day.

What It Is

Good nutrition is essential for all physiological processes, not just those associated with stress. All body systems are connected, so upsetting one will impact many others. As a result, people under stress sometimes overindulge in the one behavior they must engage in just to stay alive, eating. The desire to seek pleasure through food may be driven by appetite-enhancing chemicals or by the fact that certain foods may remind us of pleasant family gatherings and holidays. Sweet foods, especially, work in multiple ways, including the activation of pleasure centers in the brain.

Food and mood go hand in hand. What you eat can profoundly influence your mood, and your mood can shape your choices about what to eat. For example, many people feel sleepy soon after eating a lot of carbohydrates in the form of a spaghetti or lasagna dinner. The mechanism involves a rise in the sleep-inducing neurotransmitter serotonin following a meal with a high ratio of carbohydrate to protein.[46] On the other hand, many people, when stressed, turn to dessert or fatty foods. That's because these foods induce changes in the brain that temporarily make you feel good and dampen the stress response. No wonder they're called comfort foods![47]

It's not complicated. All this and more are part of the Eat It Up Lifestyle Strategy of Stress Recovery, and it really helps.

The Science Behind It

When under distress, the body may start craving rich foods because it believes there is a need for additional calories to fuel the fight-or-flight response. It works like this: You feel stress, so your body prepares itself to fight or flee. The brain dispatches chemicals to increase your desire to consume vast amounts of refined carbohydrates, which can rapidly be converted into glucose. Then glucose gives you the energy you need to take action.

A drop in the neurochemical serotonin is responsible for our carbohydrate craving. When serotonin is reduced in the brain, it can also trigger depression and sleep loss. However, under some circumstances, eating carbohydrates can restore serotonin to normal levels, thereby improving mood and sleep.

Distress can trigger a drop in serotonin, which can result in increased irritability and aggression, insomnia, and depression. Excessive stress and associated emotions such as fear and anger set the entire cascade in motion. Anything you can do to better handle stress will be of benefit. That includes eating more carbohydrates with a small amount of protein, albeit within reason. The consumption of carbohydrates will also help reduce the entire stress response. Here's how it works:

You need protein to make serotonin—specifically, an amino acid called tryptophan. But tryptophan has a limited ability to enter the brain due to other amino acids competing for the same entry points. Eating carbohydrates basically wipes out the competition, allowing tryptophan to enter. Many carbohydrates are easily converted to sugar, which triggers the release of insulin. Insulin transports blood sugar into cells where it can be used for energy or stored as glycogen in organs such as the liver. It also facilitates the transport of many amino acids into cells, where they are used to make new protein. But tryptophan is minimally affected by this property of insulin. That means when the competition is out of the way, tryptophan can slip into the brain where it can be made into serotonin. Theoretically, this could lessen depression, irritability, insomnia, and of course the craving for carbohydrates which set the whole process in motion.[48]

How to Do It

When you realize there are actions you can take reduce your stress symptoms, you'll also recognize that you can exert a measure of control over events, even those causing the stress. As noted in other chapters, having a sense of control is, by itself, a highly effective way to better manage your stress response. When you take control of eating, you are well on your way to enjoying the state of good health and well-being you so richly deserve.

1. Keep a daily log.

To help you better understand the connection between food and stress in your life, try this exercise: For one week starting today, write down everything you eat on a daily basis. Log everything including beverages. Record the amount, the time of day, your mood, and quality of sleep the previous night. Be sure to include any stressors you might be experiencing.

After a week, look for trends. You'll realize that, like many others, you may prefer carbohydrates on those days when you are experiencing more stress than usual. Not only that, but on days after you got less sleep, you most likely ate more. That's because the brain assumes that if you're awake, you're active and therefore in need of extra calories to fuel that activity.

For many people, eating energy-dense foods that load up fat cells is a normal response to distress. One of the most effective ways to break the stress-eating response is to simply be aware of what you do automatically as a habit. *For example, you may discover you reach for a snack at certain times of the day. If so, make sure you have a piece of fruit handy or a small amount of nuts instead of candy from the vending machine.* You'll also see rough spots in your diet where feelings, rather than your thoughts, drive your choices.

2. Go plant-based.

Walk through the checkout aisle of your grocery store and you'll see magazines filled with the latest diet fads. Some are supported by evidence while others reflect unfounded beliefs. Be wary of those claiming their recommendations will work for everyone. One size doesn't fit all, with lifestyle, cultural, and personal factors influencing the food choices we make. It's not as complicated as many experts make it seem. Current research points to a plant-based diet as the foundation for optimal health. You don't have to become a vegetarian; simply increase the amount of legumes, fruits, vegetables, grains, and nuts while decreasing meat and dairy products.

This diet provides a healthy ratio of omega-3 to omega-6 fatty acids and a variety of antioxidants. It's also a diet correlated with decreased depression and inflammation-based diseases.[49, 50, 51]

3. Cut back on caffeine.

To reduce feelings of stress and anxiety, cut back on or eliminate caffeine, whether in coffee, sodas, or over-the-counter medications. There are many sources of caffeine, and many are not obvious. Be careful not to quit caffeine cold turkey, especially if you are prone to migraine headaches. This may not be a medical issue, but for some it can be very annoying. If you are prone to stress and anxiety, cutting back on or eliminating caffeine may not cause your symptoms to disappear entirely, but they will become more easily managed.

4. Be carb-conscious.

Remember, stress can trigger a drop in serotonin, resulting in increased irritability, aggression, insomnia, and depression, as well as creating a craving for carbohydrates. During times of high stress, consume healthy carbs to help restore serotonin to normal levels and reduce the stress response.

Healthy carbs include:

- ⊙ Fruit

- ⊙ Whole-grain breads

- ⊙ Non-sugary cereals

- ⊙ Whole-grain pasta

- ⊙ Brown rice

- ⊙ Baked potato with skin; sweet potato

- ⊙ Quinoa

- ⊙ Oats

- ⊙ Buckwheat

Recall the last time you were under a great deal of pressure. That was probably the day you had an irresistible urge to visit the all-you-can-eat pasta bar at the local Italian restaurant or stop by the pastry shop on your way home. You were responding to brain signals urging you to self-medicate by consuming carbohydrates.

The consumption of simple carbohydrates has been found to blunt the entire stress response under some circumstances when extreme stress is occurring. Marathon runners and those undergoing excessive stress during training for specialized military units are more prone to upper respiratory infections than the general population. The immune system can be nudged back into the healthy midrange, allowing it to more effectively neutralize the microbial triggers of infection following the consumption of liquid carbohydrates.[52] But be careful. This practice has been shown to be an effective strategy only for those competing in extreme endurance activities or during arduous training by elite military units. In addition, laboratory studies have revealed that carbohydrates in the form of glucose can blunt the stress response including brain chemistry and cortisol.[53, 54] No wonder people crave carbohydrates during stress. Not only is the desire driven by a chemical change in the brain, but the reward of experiencing less stress may independently motivate the practice.

Of course, too much of a good thing can become a problem. Some people consume too much simple carbohydrate during stress, especially when the stress is accompanied by depression. Indeed, a change in eating habits (either increased or decreased eating) is part of the diagnostic criteria for depression. And consuming more calories than one can use will eventually lead to obesity and metabolic syndrome, which is capable of shortening one's life span through a number of chronic illnesses. The key is to not lose control.

A little exercise can take the edge off your appetite, so the next time you experience the urge to chow down, try walking up some stairs or walking briskly for five minutes. Many people turn to specific herbs for stress reduction (ginseng, for example). While there is some limited evidence that this and other plant-based interventions may work, its efficacy is probably greatly enhanced because the person believes it will.[55, 56] As is true of many alternative options that have not been evaluated extensively, this benefit may also be due to the placebo effect. If you think it's going to help you, then chances are it will.

Fads will come and go, but you never outgrow the basics when it comes to eating and drinking your way to a successful stress recovery program. There's no need to overthink this. The science is there; all you need to do is make healthy choices and add the Eat It Up Lifestyle Strategy to your stress recovery toolbox.

LIFESTYLE STRATEGY #7: GIVE IT A REST
Taking Intentional Breaks for Ultimate Performance

In your long-term stress recovery strategy, three approaches to "rest" will make a huge difference in managing your stressors and empowering you to get the most out of life:

1. Sleep On It

2. Take It Off

3. Switch It Up

1. Sleep On It

We live in a society that prides itself on being overworked and underslept. Being exhausted is a merit badge we wear with a twisted sense of pride. We brag about not getting enough sleep and then complain about the negative impacts on our health. (There's substantial evidence that sleep deprivation increases the incidence of obesity, diabetes, high blood pressure, depression, arthritis, and even Alzheimer's disease.[57] It also increases the rate of traffic and work-related accidents.[58])

In short, low sleep = higher stress. This added stressor can trigger a vicious cycle where the increased stress makes it harder to sleep, the less sleep you get the more stress you experience, and that added stress makes it harder to sleep. Round and round it goes. How do you break that cycle? Let's consider a typical scenario:

You come home from work all stressed out. Your mind is spinning from the work you left at the office, so you try to relax by turning on the TV or checking in on Facebook. This usually bombards your mind with more negativity and drama. To compound the effect, the blue light from your computer screen overstimulates the cones in your eyes, which further deters sleep.[59] So what do you do? You probably take that negativity and blue light into the bedroom with you. Lying in bed, you watch the television or check the news online. This is one of the worst things you can do; you are bombarding yourself with more bad news and conflict, which triggers the stress response further. Not only that, the constantly changing topics keep your brain on high alert as it bounces around from thought to thought. And, again, you are bombarding your brain with more blue light—a natural signal telling your body to wake up.

The solution? Create some fresh new habits right before bedtime that will increase your propensity to sleep.

⊙   Go to bed at about the same time every night and wake up at the same time every morning. This helps to set a better sleep pattern by associating the time of day with falling asleep. Basically, you're doing with the time of day what Pavlov did with a bell when he conditioned his dogs to salivate.

- ⊙ Have a simple three- to five-step routine that you always do right before you get in bed (e.g., check on children, brush teeth). This will help signal to your brain that it is time to sleep.

- ⊙ Eat a moderate meal at least three hours before going to bed. Our great-grandparents may have had it right when breakfast was their largest meal, followed by lunch, and finally supper being the smallest meal.

- ⊙ Drink wisely before turning in. If you drink something warm before going to bed, you may fall asleep faster. Some people believe that an alcoholic "nightcap" might help them fall asleep, but research shows that alcohol degrades the quality of sleep for the rest of the night.[60] And, of course, whatever you drink, if you drink too much you are going to have to get up in the middle of the night to get rid of it.

- ⊙ Update to-do lists early in the evening so your brain can stop reminding you of everything you need to do tomorrow.

- ⊙ Write blessings you are thankful for in a "gratitude journal."

- Read something relaxing.

- Keep your bedroom at an ideal temperature between 65° and 70°.

- Take a hot shower, sauna, or hot bath. Your body will react to this by *lowering* your body temperature for a short time after you step out, thereby slowing your metabolism and helping you calm down. A hot drink before bedtime will have the same effect if, of course, you avoid caffeine.

- Dim the lights a minimum of one hour before you want to fall asleep. This tells your body that it really is nighttime and time to shut down. And make sure your curtains block out the light trying to come in through your window.

- Don't look at your computer, TV, smartphone, or any other electronic device that emits a blue light at least a full hour before going to bed. For some this will be the hardest thing to do, but blue light stimulates the cones of your eyes, making it more difficult to sleep.

- Short naps during the day are also recommended. Fifteen to twenty minutes between one and three p.m. increases alertness, performance, and creative thinking while lowering levels of perceived stress. But don't overdo it. Naps are problematic for some people. Sleeping too much during the day may make it harder to sleep at night.[61]

What if all this fails to work and you are lying in bed, trying to fall asleep, looking at the clock tick away minute after minute, and all you can think is, *I'm going to be a zombie tomorrow!*

- ⊙ Get out of bed. You don't want your brain to associate your bed with sleeplessness and worry. If it does, you may automatically start sleepless worry just by getting in bed.

- ⊙ Do several of the Stress Response Strategies from chapter 4.

- ⊙ Sit in one of the least comfortable chairs in the house. You don't want to associate your favorite and most comfortable chair with the worry cycle and ruminating about sleeplessness.

- ⊙ Get the worrying out of the way. Worrying is not bad; it's higher processing. You're reflecting on what has happened and figuring out possible solutions. So get up and go to your "worry space" if possible.

- ⊙ Mentally rehearse what you want tomorrow to be like. Your calm space is a great place to do this. But put a limit on the number of rehearsals you will do. You don't want this to go on all night!

- ⊙ Read something tedious but easy to read. Think of a catalog, such as a seed catalog or an office supply catalog.

- ⊙ Go back to bed with a clear mind and a restful heart and sleep on it.

2. Take It Off

Yes, we all wish we had more time. It would be great to have an extra day between Saturday and Sunday... or would it? Wouldn't we just fill it up with more activity? Maybe the solution is not having more time; maybe we just need 1) better priorities and 2) better practices for using the time we do have more wisely. This is where the "go slower to go faster" maxim really makes sense. We are big proponents of taking off one full day per week.

For the past thirty years, Nick has regularly incorporated at least one day per week into his schedule for pure reflection. It started when he was running a research lab during the early phase of his research career. He was competing for federal grants and under tremendous pressure to perform under the "publish-or-perish" mentality of high-stakes academia. While his colleagues at the university were slaving away in the laboratories and at their desks, Nick would take time to go to the beach or go for long rides on his bicycle. During those times he found that his mind was freed up to think outside the box, to ponder connections and relationships between biological systems, and arrive at unique solutions to the scientific questions he faced. Taking time away from the lab created a space where his brain could work naturally without the constraints of pressure. He was building a natural stress recovery time into his life. His overall productivity increased significantly because of this habit.

There's something about taking a day off that kick-starts the creativity of complex cognitive activity. Dick takes a full day off each week as part of his religious practice of worship. When others are filling their Saturdays with golf, shopping, or any of a long list of activities, Dick experiences community by gathering with like-minded believers at church and finds renewal and fellowship in afternoon walks and visits with family and friends. There is a reason the Bible suggests a day of worship once a week. In fact, studies of Seventh-day Adventists in Loma Linda, California—the only "Blue Zone" in the United States (Blue Zones are regions in the world where residents live longer and healthier than average)[62]—demonstrate that people who take one day a week for reflection, rest, and recharge often live longer, healthier, and more fulfilling lives than those who don't. Taking a weekly day off also puts you in sync with circaseptum rhythms, the seven-day cycles programmed into humans.

3. Switch It Up

Most people consider "rest" as inactivity, taking a break and doing very little. What if you switched that up? What if you did something for others in order to do something for you? Is it possible that, if you reorganized your life a little, you might get a rest from your stressors while helping others with the issues that cause them distress?

Altruism is the belief in or practice of selfless concern and sacrifice for the well-being of others. Altruism is a spiritual principle of giving without expecting anything in return. And yet there seems to be a different set of economics at work within the soul. The saying "It is better to give than to receive" does hold true when it comes to altruism.

The fact is, we live in a world full of need, and each of us has an abundance of resources in certain areas. When we invest those resources in others, we gain significant personal dividends in return; we get rest and a reprieve from many of the factors that cause us distress.

Nick recently spent a week doing volunteer work in Honduras. It was not all fun, but it was very rewarding. Working on several Rotary International–sponsored projects in remote and primitive areas, he and the team helped develop a shelter for girls who had been rescued from the sex trade. They also put in water wells for villages and helped build a school. If you voluntarily spend some time in primitive conditions, your perspective changes on what you have and what it's like to live involuntarily without the things we so often take for granted.

Having a cause outside of ourselves is perhaps the most powerful way to reframe our current circumstances and get a rest from the stressors that plague us. One of the benefits of standing in the serving line at a soup kitchen is that you don't spend much time there wishing you had a bigger house and newer car or being frustrated that your brother-in-law got a raise and you didn't. Serving others who lack even the essentials puts your own life in perspective.

Altruism may be the principle of giving without expecting anything in return, but it has a boomerang effect. Through our giving, we unleash a powerful stress recovery Lifestyle Strategy. How do you start to Switch It Up like this?

Ponder your personal skills and resources. What are you good at? What do you like to do? Where do you have abundance in your life?

Open your eyes to the needs of others around you.

Find the intersection between your skills and passions and the needs of others.

Take a step of action into that need, and test whether this becomes a blessing back to you. It will.

In your long-term stress recovery strategy, the three approaches to "rest" will make a huge difference in recovering from your stressors and empowering you to get the most out of life. If you Sleep On It, Take It Off, and Switch It Up, you'll find that these intentional reprieves from normal life and never-ending work lead to empowered engagement for the rest of your life.

"One hand full of rest is better than two fists full of labor and striving after wind."
—KING SOLOMON

LIFESTYLE STRATEGY IMPLEMENTATIONS

Integrating the Lifestyle Strategies leverages powerful tools in your stress recovery toolbox.

If you want to start using a particular Lifestyle Strategy right now, we are all for it. But start slow. It's always tempting to start too many strategies too fast and do too much. For now, pick *one* Lifestyle Strategy. Just one. And choose one that is fairly easy for you.

At the back of the book, we have included a Weekly Planner that will help you start incorporating the strategies into your daily routine.

Great! You have the tools and you're already starting to use them.

- ☉ Seven Response Strategies in your top tray for immediate and emergency use.

- ☉ Seven Lifestyle Strategies in the bottom of your toolbox to build a better future.

In Part 3 we will explore more power principles that will leverage your efforts for maximum stress recovery.

STRESSED-OUT STUDENTS

Can The Stress Recovery Effect *Curriculum Help College Students?*

Nick Hall

he Stress Recovery Effect program was initially developed as an employee wellness curriculum and tested in a high-stress healthcare work environment. The positive feedback we received from participants over the course of five years clearly showed that the strategies described in *The Stress Recovery Effect* curriculum are highly effective in alleviating stress in that setting. Of the nearly 5,000 people who took the course:

- ⊙ 90% said it made them aware of methods to recover from stress, and

- ⊙ 74% said they had learned strategies to better recover from stress.

The IRB (Institutional Review Board) research study we conducted confirmed a statistically significant benefit among curriculum study participants as well. Results compiled from follow-up questionnaires revealed that:

⊙ 100% of participants adopted stress recovery strategies they learned from the course,

⊙ 98% of study participants felt better equipped to manage their stress, and

⊙ 79% of study participants found the course very or extremely helpful.

WHAT ABOUT IN ACADEMIA?

Is it possible to take a program that was developed in a high-octane, busy clinical work environment to academia? We knew *The Stress Recovery Effect* worked in a healthcare setting. Could learning its strategies help students recover from the stresses they faced in their academic environment as well? As one of the authors of the program, I decided to put the question to the test.

I planned a strategy to convey the stress-management principles of *The Stress Recovery Effect* curriculum with pre-nursing Anatomy and Physiology (A&P) students. Participation was voluntary and offered as an extra-credit assignment. Prior to starting, students were required to complete a questionnaire describing those things they found stressful, both before and after entering college. A similar questionnaire seeking their feedback about the curriculum was completed at the end of the semester. Then, I shared with the entire class the self-guided workbook of *The Stress Recovery Effect* on the A&P course website. After an introduction to the concepts of stress recovery, participating students completed a series of open-ended questions with no word-count limit:

WHAT'S ON YOUR MIND?

Identify the stressors in your life—past, present, and future. Describe what happened and how you felt.

- ⊙ *What stressors you are experiencing at this time? Include those pertaining to both your personal and academic life. What makes them stressful?*

- ⊙ *What did you find most stressful prior to starting high school, and then during high school?*

- ⊙ *What do you anticipate will be your greatest form of stress in the future? Include only those things you have already thought about.*

- ⊙ *What did or do you find to be an effective strategy in reducing your stress? Do you do it on a regular basis?*

SMARTPHONES, DISTRACTIONS, AND STRESS

In addition to providing a copy of the *Stress Recovery Effect* workbook, I provided the students with an article entitled "Tune Your Brain." Research reviewing the adverse effects of cell phone use upon cognitive function was summarized. For example, data collected by Apple reveals that, on average, a person uses their smartphone 80 times a day. One study that sought to test the effect of a smartphone on intellectual acuity, divided its subjects into three groups. One group kept their phones in front of them, another group put their phones in their purses or pockets, and a third group placed their phones in another room. The collective research substantiated what many people have suspected: "As the phone's proximity increased, brainpower decreased." Consequently, the students were instructed as follows:

1. Never have your phone present in a classroom or study area—leave it outside the room or if that's not practical, place it in the bottom of a purse or bag.

2. If you are completing an online assignment, use your computer and not your phone. Then, temporarily inactivate any access to messaging services or social media. It's the anticipation of a call or an abrupt interruption that disrupts your concentration.

3. Keep your phone out of sight when studying a difficult subject.

4. Decide on specific times during the day when you will use your smartphone.

For the following two days, I instructed them to study in their regular manner but to keep track of the number of times they checked their phones for messages or logged on to social media, and the quality of their study time. They were to score from 1 to 10 how the study sessions felt to them. On the third day, they were to leave their phones off and in another room—or at least stored out of sight—while studying. Then, they were to assess the quality of their study sessions and report their results for the three days. If the quality of their study sessions improved, I instructed them to distance themselves from their smartphones.

As their final assignment, students answered another series of questions:

1. Reflect upon your answers to the questions you answered in the first assignment (early, current, future stressors). Now describe how completing *The Stress Recovery Effect* program has affected the way you view the subject of stress.

2. If you believe the program has helped you better cope with stress, please describe how and which specific parts of the program proved most helpful. If you don't believe it helped, why? What would have been useful? Perhaps you're already employing strategies that have kept your level of stress at a minimum all along. If so, what are those strategies?

3. Do you believe the strategies have improved your study skills and ability to learn the material not only in Anatomy and Physiology, but other courses as well?

The stressors reported by the students before starting the program covered a variety of categories. Fear of failure in the classroom was at the top of the list followed closely by financial concerns. All the reported stressors are listed below from greatest to least:

1. Fear of failure
2. Financial concerns
3. Online course format
4. Fatigue
5. High family expectations (this was noted primarily by a number of Asian students)
6. Relationships with peers
7. Limited socialization due to COVID restrictions
8. Anger issues
9. Health concerns
10. Concerns about what others think of them
11. Body weight concerns
12. Uncertainty about the future
13. Care giving responsibilities involving family members

14. Finding a partner

15. Roommate disputes

16. Work related stress

Fifty-five of the seventy-six students completed the assignment. Based on their responses, achieving the objective of helping students better cope with their stressors was highly successful. The very positive written evaluations revealed that nearly all the students who participated found the protocols extremely valuable. Some brief quotes from the student responses serve as examples:

> *"One of the response strategies that really helped me was pausing what I'm doing and stretching out; it gives me a moment to relax and refocus my thoughts."*

> *"Since completing the stress recovery effect program, I have developed a stronger mindset and better tools for dealing with my constant stressors."*

> *"I really appreciate this program and the skills that it taught me to better function not only professionally and as a student, but personally as well."*

> *"I feel that this program has really allowed me to feel more comfortable being uncomfortable. I feel that managing my stress has become easier with sticking to my workout, work, and school routine."*

"Finishing the stress recovery program has influenced my view on stress because it encouraged me to think about my stressors in the long term rather than the short-term stressors I have right in front of me."

"The Stress Recovery [Effect] program allowed me to learn new ways to work through the different ways and reasons why I experience stress. I learned that completely getting rid of my stress is unrealistic but learning new ways to cope with stress is crucial."

"Thank you from the bottom of my heart for this chance to look deeply into my own environment. By giving me this assignment, you have blessed my life more that you will ever know. I love the "breathe it out, stretch it, laugh it up, and rock it." The last one is new to me. That is how I calm my own children when they are overwhelmed with anything; however, I never knew that this simple technique has great results with grownups too!"

"My level of stress has become manageable, and I feel more successful than last semester.... Thank you so much for this great opportunity to become a better parent, student, and human being. Please know that I am doing well in my other classes. I am completing things in time and on time. I have much hope for the semesters ahead of me."

"Since I've started this [Stress Recovery Effect] approach, my episodes of heightened stress have decreased along with the duration of each episode."

"While I am still working on managing my reactions and responses to stress, this program has greatly opened my eyes to better understand the connection among stress, responses, and future perspective."

"I have always had stress but never a real understanding of what it is and how to direct it. This program has taught me skills that will transcend into many areas of my life."

"This program allowed me to do in-depth inward searching and realize that I'm not the only one experiencing these feelings and that through proper strategies these stressors can actually be positive things."

CONCLUSION

Many students found the strategies they learned of immeasurable value, both academically and personally. The program especially seems beneficial because it helps students assess their current stress levels, identify their stressors, and systematically improve the stressors in their lives. Most surprising was their feedback regarding cell phones. Multiple students acknowledged their cell phones were a distraction, both during the study period and immediately after when it prevented full assimilation of the previous learned material. Those students who heeded the advice to remove their phones from the learning environment reported a marked improvement in their ability to learn the material.

This pilot research project was undertaken to assess whether the Stress Recovery Effect program along with supplemental information would improve students' academic performance. The approach adopted to assess improvement relied upon open-ended, written self-reports. While this format did not lend itself to the use of traditional statistical analyses, it did confirm how a program designed for workers in a high-pressure healthcare environment can be realized in a comparable high-pressure academic environment. It's anticipated that similar benefits can be experienced in virtually any high-stakes environment.

PART 3

UNLEASHING THE POTENTIAL

"Know thyself."

—Greek Maxim Inscribed on
The Temple of Apollo at Delphi

To get deep into the Optimal Zone, we need to know ourselves and examine our lives to make them really worth living. This is what Part 3 is all about. We're going to dig deep, do a lot of self-discovery, and create a plan to proactively recover from your stressors and center your life in the Optimal Zone.

Socrates, while on trial for corrupting youth (by teaching them how to think), proclaimed, "The unexamined life is not worth living." Another Greek maxim was "Know thyself."

What do these two Greek philosophies have to do with stress recovery? Plenty. Part 2 was all about the tools you have available to deal with acute stressors in the moment and managing your lifestyle with long-term strategies that really help. Progressive muscle relaxation, mindfulness, deep breathing... All these strategies help manage stressors, but they only address the *symptoms*.

If we don't know ourselves and understand how we work, we're just putting a Band-Aid on those symptoms. Band-Aids help temporarily, but they are no help in coming up with long-term solutions to the root causes, and they can't make us holistically vibrant and healthy. The principles in the next three chapters, however, can.

We're going to unlock little-known techniques that get you working *with* your physiology and *with* your personal psychology rather than *against* them. This, in turn, unleashes the potential of the Stress Recovery Effect, a potent mixture of Key Principles we've been talking about so far:

Key Principle #1: Manage What You Can Control

Key Principle #2: Go Slower to Go Faster

In chapter 6, the main takeaway will be strategic, proactive steps to turbocharge your stress management efforts. It illuminates theory and application, giving understanding and exercises to manage what you can control. We will focus on the physical, mental, and emotional so you come away with a holistic, balanced perspective.

Chapter 7 pulls together everything you've been learning and applying throughout this book. By going slower to go faster, we will integrate Recovery Strategies, Lifestyle Strategies, the Optimal Zone, and the Stress Recovery Effect into a single model with a simple and powerful plan of action you can customize for your own personality and purposes.

In the last chapter, we will give you two more Key Principles to help you be victorious:

Key Principle #3: Look Farther Down the Track

Key Principle #4: Life Is Best When We Live for Something Beyond Ourselves

Chapter 8 is about the power of habit transformation, vision, and mission. This will bring us full circle so you can tap into the natural design of who you were meant to be. Living one day at a time may help when we are feeling overwhelmed, but it can also serve as a trap to keep us stuck in our daily existence. Dick always teaches his racers to look farther than what is right in front of them. By looking farther down the track, they can set themselves up for success in the race and make better decisions in the moment. We too need to "look down the track" with a sense of purpose and destiny. Life is not just about where we are today but where we see ourselves tomorrow, next month, next year, and ultimately at the end of our life. We will introduce our final maxim there: "Life is best when we live for something beyond ourselves."

TAKING CHARGE

*Managing What You Can Control Through
the Stress Recovery Effect*

NICK HALL: IN HARM'S WAY, PART 1

They were perhaps some of the darkest days in the history of the Western world. As millions of innocents were being railroaded to their deaths on the ground, hell was being unleashed from the skies upon London. The mental and physical distress was incalculable as countless lives were destroyed by the Nazi bombers that dropped their fury every night. In my homeland of England, a mass exodus away from the carnage swept the majority of women and children to Ireland— to get them out of the country so they could repopulate England, because everybody assumed the Germans would eventually invade. My mother was just eighteen and could have fled. But her skills were needed in the greater war. By day she worked for an oil company; at night the bombs fell. Each morning she walked to *work amid the smoldering buildings, around the bodies covered with tarps. At the office, she counted the empty desks, knowing those coworkers didn't make it through the night.*

I have recordings of her experience. She talks about hearing the sirens go off but not bothering to go down to the bomb shelter because she was just too tired. And then the next morning... she would repeat the walk to work. And the next morning, and the next, and the next...

She literally walked "through the valley of the shadow of death" day after day.

Thankfully for her (and luckily for me, her yet-to-be-born son), she survived and took her place in what Tom Brokaw called "The Greatest Generation." And not only that, she was also one of the most upbeat, resilient people I have ever met. How could that be?

AFTER THE WAR

Fast-forward seventy years. Although terrorism and mass shootings are an ongoing nebulous threat, the large-scale global conflicts are all taking place on foreign shores away from the Western world. Except for the handful of women and men who put themselves in harm's way in those distant lands, the rest of us in the West generally live in homes that are safe, with refrigerators full of food, and—thanks to Maslow—self-actualization is our biggest concern.

Yet here's an interesting generalization: The people who've grown up very protected, who have never experienced any adversity, are the ones who fall apart the easiest. We see that in our clients and in our students. Nick has university students come to him because they got a B on an exam, and they're almost in tears. "I've never gotten a grade less than an A before!" If one of Dick's motorsport clients does poorly in a race, they sometimes exhibit intense anger or despair. We are all so much alike, aren't we? We are all similar to the student and the motorsport professional. It's not who you are or what you do—it's how you handle the stress that matters.

So how did we get to this place? Some people say, "Stress: You can't live with it, and you can't live without it." In our professions, we are engaged with both ends of this statement. Most of the people we work with desire to eliminate as much stress from their lives as possible. Perhaps this describes you too. But the premier athletes we coach actively seek stressors to perform at the highest level of their sport. Want to become WWII tough? You will perform at your best not by *eliminating* all stressors from your life but rather by *recovering more effectively* from the stressors you do have.

"Between stimulus and response there is a space. In that space is our power to choose our response. In our response lies our growth and our freedom."
—VIKTOR FRANKL

Many people endure distress (the potentially harmful form of stress). However, they seldom take time to teach themselves to recover from it. Events giving rise to distress may well be outside your control, but recovery is in your hands.

Our parents (or grandparents) and the toughest members of their generation became that way after enduring the Great Depression and the consequences of a world war. After surviving those years of death and uncertainty, nothing seemed to faze them. The distress and adversity they endured didn't break them. It made many of them stronger. Later, when faced with hardship, they knew they had recovered from far worse circumstances. From that perspective, nothing seemed quite as bad. Some, however, fell into deep states of depression or committed suicide. What are the characteristics of those who found ways to thrive under extreme stressors? Can we use their coping strategies as we deal with lesser amounts of stressors? We believe the answer is yes.

In this chapter, we are going to turbo-charge your ability to recover from stressors. By strategically injecting eustress (the constructive form of stress) into your system, you will learn a technique that will enable your body and brain to automatically recover from distress. No, we aren't going to send you into a war zone. However, we are going to train you to manage what you can control so you can recover better and faster from any stressors that come your way, whether controllable or not.

In our battle against distress, so often we feel like we are always on the defense. As the "bombs" fall around us, we try to protect ourselves, to divert catastrophe away from us. We say, "Enough of that."

It's time to go on the offense.

It's time to use your outer brain to think this through.

What we are proposing is this:

You have a chance to inject positive eustress into your life in a way that strengthens your whole being so you can handle more distress and spend more time in the Optimal Zone.

Remember the Bell Curve graph with the Optimal Zone of stressors? You can actually change the size of your Optimal Zone, and this will change your life. How? By training yourself to adapt and handle more intense stressors.

Untrained Optimal Zone

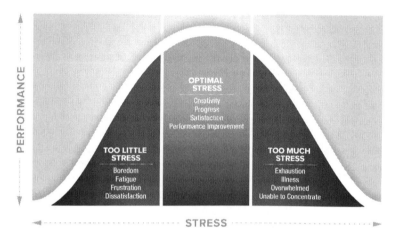

Expand Your Optimal Zone

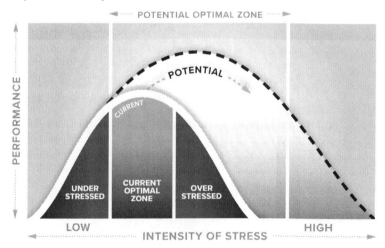

It's time to not only survive but to thrive. We get tired of simply making it through. We believe life was designed to be more than survival. It's time to play to win. It's time to be proactive rather than simply reactive. Play defense against distress? Of course, you will want to reduce the many stressors in your life. But it's a lot more rewarding and beneficial to call the shots and take on life's challenges, recovering more quickly from whatever comes your way.

Start by thinking of the neuronal connections in the brain as the hardware of a computer. The software is made up of all your experiences and education. Both the hardware and software make us unique. Here's the important part, and this is key: You can become the computer programmer of your own brain and body by tapping into established physiological and psychological principles. In short, the Stress Recovery Effect:

1. Trains your body to recover faster from *any* stressor.

2. Trains your mind to implement Stress Recovery Strategies automatically.

You can:

1. Take control—to a large degree—of the way you perceive triggers and therefore how you will respond to them.

2. Intentionally program in new triggers that are linked to healthy and beneficial responses.

3. Adapt a proactive attitude and approach to train your brain and body.

No, you can't control everything. There are always those pesky drivers sliding into your lane. There are always the unexpected pink slips and "Dear John" letters. And we can't slow down time, either. But, in the midst of all that, there are important and essential variables we can control—*if* we choose to.

INJECTING EUSTRESS

Here is the major factor you *can* control:

By intentionally and repeatedly bathing the body's cells in stress hormones through physical, mental, and emotional exercises, the cells experience recovery and become better adapted to stress. By strategically injecting doses of healthy eustress, the cells learn to recover faster. Then, when adversity triggers the stress response, these cells are better able to return to healthy levels.

Trained Stress Recovery

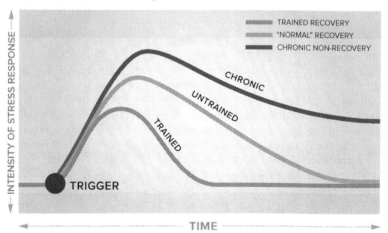

PHYSICALLY INDUCED EUSTRESS

Physical exercise will induce many of the same changes associated with stress, minus the harmful ones. For example:

- ⊙ Your heart will beat faster.

- ⊙ Your lungs will work harder.

- ⊙ Your skin will become damp with perspiration.

There's a reason why athletes intentionally and strategically seek out stressors to improve performance. You can do the same to improve your stress response fitness.

This means you can use physical exercise as eustress to train your body and brain to be more resilient and to recover faster from distress.

What's the best kind of exercise? That's up to you.

- ⊙ What do you like to do the most? Hike hills? Kayak rivers? Liking some type of physical exercise is the most important element. If you don't like it, you won't do it. If you like it, you'll get out and do it!

- ⊙ Whom do you like to do it with? Friends, family, or just yourself?

- ⊙ Where is the best place? Stairwell of your office building? A gym? The park?

Just make sure you *like* it. Anything that gets the heart pumping and is fun to you will do the job.

Potential Sources of Physical Eustressors

- ⊙ Walking, running, sprinting

- ⊙ Cycling, indoor or outdoor

- ⊙ Push-ups, sit-ups, pull-ups (and anything else that "ups," like dips, squats, lunges, burpees, etc.)

- ⊙ Swimming

- ⊙ Kickboxing

- ⊙ Zumba

- ⊙ CrossFit

- ⊙ Mixed Martial Arts

- ⊙ Spinning

The list goes on and on! Just pick something you like; do it in a place you like with people you enjoy!

MENTALLY INDUCED EUSTRESS

We now know that the mental, physical, and spiritual aspects of our lives are inseparably intertwined. Two factors affect heart rate and stress response: activities and thoughts. Activity obviously modulates heart rate, but thoughts do too.

Think about this important concept for a moment: We cannot objectively measure a stressor's strength in triggering the stress response. Why? Because it's based on individual *perception*. Remember, it's the *perception* of the stressor that triggers the stress response.

One person can perceive something as an energizing challenge; another might become overwhelmed and paralyzed by it. The difference is all in the mind—and what's going on in your head is extremely complex. That's why we have been principle-driven in this book rather than giving you formulas, because the characteristics of each person's Optimal Zone is absolutely unique.

If you use exercises to train your body to respond to your activities *and* thoughts, you're now in control of the two major variables that drive the stress response.

This means you can use mental exercise as eustress to train your body and brain to be more resilient and to recover faster from distress.

Athletes do this all the time. They call it visualization or mental imagery. They picture the activity they are about to do over and over in their mind until it becomes imprinted in the neuromuscular pathways associated with the activity. Then when they go out to do the real thing, it is not as stressful because their body has mentally rehearsed it hundreds of times.

If something upsets you, your heart rate goes up. If you think about something that's pleasant, your heart rate can go down. Remember, it's our *perception* of events that triggers the stress response. If you have a heart rate monitor on throughout the day, you'll notice that just thinking about bothersome issues will cause your heart rate to go up.

Dick not only wires his clients to heart monitors, he monitors his own heart rate on a regular basis. Like the rest of us, he prefers to stay in the Optimal Zone as much as possible to do his best work. He has learned that even if he's just sitting at his computer sending emails, or thinking about what he needs to do later, his heart rate can creep up. He may not even be aware of what he is thinking, but depending on if his thoughts are positive or negative, his heart rate can creep up or go down outside of his awareness.

Increased heart rate is a reminder to him that something is building up in his thoughts. He can use one of the intervention strategies to release it. But if he doesn't, his heart rate can climb out of his Optimal Zone, even though he's just sitting and not doing anything physical. If he doesn't use Stress Response Strategies throughout the day, he comes home with tight shoulders, a bit of a headache, and lots of tension. It creeps up on him, just as it creeps up on all of us. It's like the water temperature going up one degree at a time. You don't notice it until it gets too hot. The heart rate monitor, like a thermometer, will let you know earlier. If your heart rate goes up? You will know that tensions and pressures are rising somewhere. If they can be released throughout the day in small segments, you can reduce the buildup that results in the headache at the end of the day.

The impact of our mental thoughts on the stress response is both bad news and great news. Yes, chronic mental stressors can tear you up. But with physical and mental exercise in your arsenal, you control both major variables that drive heart rate and the stress response.

Here's the strategic part: It's possible to create beautiful training results using mental triggers! By injecting repeated doses of mental eustress, you train both your brain and your body to recover more quickly from the stress response.

Potential Sources of Mental Eustressors

- Board games

- Escape rooms. We haven't tried this yet, but they are the current fad in group dynamics and problem solving.

- Puzzles are abundant, and the internet is flush with challenging, fun mind games. You can compete in real time with other people. The more you get into it, the better. The goal is to inject a nice, repeated dosage of mental eustress into your system. The timing and cadence of most of these games is perfect for that.

- Mind teasers

- Mazes

- Riddles

Ideally, pick something challenging and then intensify it with competition or a time deadline. A competitive atmosphere can help get your heart rate up. More intense mental exercises can help further. Really concentrating and getting into the game helps simulate the mental stressors you face in the real world and increases your heart rate in healthy, cyclical ways that train brain and body to recover faster.

EMOTIONALLY INDUCED EUSTRESS

Two emotions get heart rate up most rapidly: anger and fear. Stress-induced emotions, especially fear, can trigger avoidance in the inner brain. We tend to avoid the stressor rather than deal with it. When that happens, you avoid not only those concerns associated with the events that give rise to your emotions but also the actions you need to be doing to recover from the stressors. By facing fear and anger, instead of avoiding these emotions, we can take charge in powerful ways.

Fear and anxiety are part of the natural stress response. When you are anxious, you generally have three options:

1.   You can avoid the concern (this will only cause your worry to reappear elsewhere and at the most unexpected times).

2.   You can remain anxious (this may paralyze you and make you even more anxious).

3.   You can address the concern (this gets the issue on the table so you can deal with it).

We are prescribing an even better option: Strategically face down your fears—and even create fearful triggers—so your body and brain can learn to handle them and recover more quickly.

You don't have to overcome your every fear. You don't have to wrestle alligators, race a motorcycle at over 100 mph on a dirt track, or jump from a high bridge tethered to a bungee cord to prove you can deal with stress. All you need to do is face your own challenges with the determination that they will not defeat you. Practice the principles outlined in this book and you will be better equipped to deal with the stressors in your life.

This means that you can use emotional exercise as eustress to train your body and brain to be more resilient and to recover faster from distress.

Nick intentionally puts people into fear-inducing activities at Saddlebrook Resort in Tampa, home to an extreme obstacle course.

This injects all three kinds of positive eustress. To test the results, Nick put heart rate monitors on the people who were climbing and the people holding the safety rope. He found interesting results. The people holding the safety ropes had higher heart rates than those who were climbing. We think that is because of the responsibility they shoulder and the lack of control they have over the ever-impending fall. Holding someone's life in your hands is a huge responsibility. That's a very emotional experience. He will then have them do a variety of activities to create cycles of increased heart rate followed by recovery to a predetermined level. After several repetitions, their stress response gradually declines, but not fully. They need a certain amount of stress to remain vigilant, but not so much that it interferes with their concentration and the task at hand, which is keeping the climber safe.

Nick once conducted a three-day training program on the emotions of stress in Las Vegas. He instructed the thirty participants to go out in pairs and do *something* to get their heart rate up. It had to be legal—by Las Vegas standards at least—and not too dangerous. One person had a terrible fear of heights. He had dinner on top of a spire with a revolving restaurant. Two women who were rule keepers and withdrawn decided to cut to the front of a very long taxi line. And they did it! (If you're from a big city, that's par for the course, but this was a huge emotional stretch for conservative Midwesterners from rural America.) The actions people came up with were routine for some and terrifying for others. When they came back and talked about their experiences, they were so overjoyed that they had stepped out of their comfort zones without any of the imagined consequences that they wanted to do it again!

The beauty of these emotional exercises is that *you* control them. *You* choose something that will cause emotional excitement for *you*. It can be anything. It may not be stressful for anyone else on the planet. But if you think it will do it for you, then do it. That's what you can do to train the emotional component in stress recovery. An emotional exercise is more difficult than physical exercise but not as difficult as constantly dealing with the health-destructive emotions of chronic stress.

If you have a keen imagination and/or excellent acting skills, you don't even have to do the exercise for real. Is it possible to use the imaginative and predictive power of the brain to achieve a similar result? To a certain extent, yes.

Years ago, Nick did a study featured on the *Healing and the Mind* series for PBS.[63] He worked with professional actors, who walked on stage with highly intense scenarios in the script. Then they were given "happy-go-lucky" scenarios to act out. They also wore heart rate monitors. The actors' bodies responded as if the scenarios were real. In this elaborate and expensive study, they also surveyed the audience to assess their level of discomfort. It was a small study, so the conclusions are limited, but conceptually and anecdotally, vividly imagining an emotionally stress-inducing situation is a sound strategy that could work for some people. It's not "fake it till you make it." Instead, an accomplished actor, like a committed athlete, will actually experience the emotion they are summoning. Dan Jansen attributes his Olympic gold medal in speed skating in part to this technique. For years leading up to the competition, he "acted" himself into a winning mindset.[64]

What do we do with all of this? Plenty! Because of the emotional impact of stressors, we can leverage the Stress Recovery Effect and use your emotions to improve your ability to respond to stressors of all kinds, particularly your emotional stressors. This requires being proactive. It means seeking out healthy eustress-inducing activities to improve your ability to recover. Here are some possibilities:

Potential Sources of Emotional Eustressors

- Ride a roller coaster
- Hold a harmless snake
- Approach a stranger
- Eat food you have never tried before
- Skydive

⊙ Rock climb

⊙ Parasail

⊙ Speak in public

⊙ Wear outlandish clothes

⊙ Bungee jump

⊙ Swim in cold water

⊙ Go to the top of a tall building in a glass elevator

⊙ Roller skate

⊙ Ride on a motorcycle

Some of these activities may be a part of your normal routine. However, for some individuals, these activities may offer an opportunity to experience what emotional distress feels like. More importantly, they learn to overcome and get over it. That's the key element.

Successfully recovering from adversity is how we learn to be optimistic. "This too shall pass" is the lesson learned. And if it's really bad, from that point on you can reflect upon the experience. When confronted with a different type of challenge, you can say to yourself, "I'm glad I'm not _____ [in cold water, bungee jumping, or whatever you did that raised your adrenaline]."

Dick loves roller coasters and the adrenaline rush that comes from the ride. His wife? Not at all. She does better with both feet firmly planted on the ground. For most of Dick's life, he would go to amusement parks to ride every roller coaster he could. His wife would prefer going to zoos and watching the wide variety of animals they contained. So when he and his wife went to Busch Gardens—thinking it was a zoo—imagine how Dick's eyes lit up when he saw all the roller coasters. Not wanting to leave his wife on this date, he talked her into riding just one coaster ride, and she agreed. So Dick picked a coaster that did loops and twists all while the floor dropped away so their feet dangled in the air. After all, he thought, if you're only going to ride one coaster, go for the biggest and baddest coaster there is!

Apparently, everyone else in the park felt this was the best coaster to ride as well, because the line was long. So there they were, standing in line as they had been doing all morning. But when Dick looked at his wife, her face was flush. He took her pulse; her heart was racing at 190 beats per minute. Why was this happening to her? They were simply standing in line. But in her mind, she was already on that coaster and it was scaring her to death. This was a vivid reminder that our body's only reality is what the mind communicates to it.

We can be as safe as possible with our feet firmly planted on the ground, but if our mind is on that coaster, it's as if our body is there as well. Notice how Dick and his wife viewed the same stressor in two very different ways. To her the roller coaster was terrifying, and to Dick it was exciting. Same coaster, two different ways of seeing it.

Nick regularly takes extreme risks, yet he hates roller coasters. But he loves his kids more than he detests roller coasters, so one day he took them on the ride inside the dark cavern of Space Mountain at Disney World. For Nick, who maintained a death grip on the safety bar, the emotional challenge was not so much the sensation of danger as it was the sense of lack of control.

What about you? What causes you emotional distress? Life is a metaphorical roller coaster ride for all of us. When something bad happens, think of it as an opportunity to practice training your cells to recover quickly from the stressor. Better yet, if you intentionally train your body with emotional eustress, you can train yourself to recover from distress in highly efficient ways.

Which of the three categories of induced eustress is most effective: physical, mental, or emotional? The answer—as you can now predict—is all three. We always recommend a full mixture of physical, mental, and emotional exercises to get the most out of the Stress Recovery Effect. Since human beings are amazingly diverse, it's best to use a diverse approach to increase the probability that your exercises will be effective for you. This diversity increases the chances that your exercise will be a good simulation for real-life stressors too. So mix it up and try all sorts of exercises from each category. That will make your responses more effective when you're staring down the real thing. And you will have a lot of fun doing it.

The Science Behind It: Classical Conditioning

Ivan Petrovich Pavlov was a Russian physiologist in the late 1800s and early 1900s who won a Nobel

Prize in 1904. He did pioneering work in pain and stress, but, ironically, he is most famous because of his dogs. His experiments showed how, with training, a random trigger could elicit an unrelated response. This has become known as classical conditioning.

Pavlov's Classical Conditioning

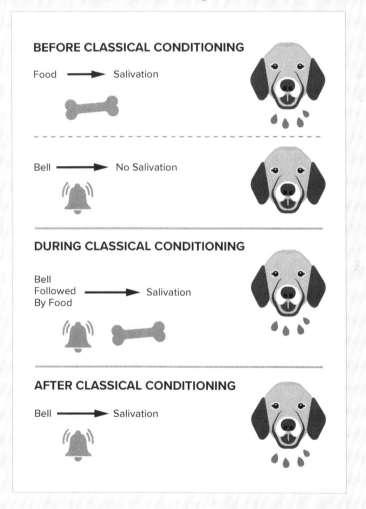

BEFORE CLASSICAL CONDITIONING

Food ⟶ Salivation

Bell ⟶ No Salivation

DURING CLASSICAL CONDITIONING

Bell Followed By Food ⟶ Salivation

AFTER CLASSICAL CONDITIONING

Bell ⟶ Salivation

Pavlov's research has had a huge influence on modern psychology by showing how our learning processes work and how habits can form.

In addition, classical conditioning is intensified when the original exposure to the stimulus is highly traumatic. A neurotransmitter called norepinephrine, which is produced in the brain stem, is released during the perception of a traumatic event. It bathes the part of the brain that puts information into memory. After a traumatic event, you can often remember every little detail surrounding the event. For example, most of us can remember exactly where we were when we heard that the World Trade Center was attacked on 9/11. In extreme situations, huge amounts of norepinephrine are released, making the memory *extremely* clear. This leaves behind a permanent memory footprint. The slightest recollection of sounds, smells, or visuals associated with the incident will elicit the full-blown image of what happened and trigger an acute stress response, as if the original event were actually taking place.[65]

Sometimes this conditioning leads to problems. For people who suffer from post-traumatic stress, for example, classical conditioning can be very difficult.

A gun (with its loud sound) ➡ acute stress reaction
Any loud sound ➡ acute stress reaction

In some cases, classical conditioning causes good intentions to backfire. For example, some cancer doctors put fish tanks in their office waiting rooms to help calm patients. But because people are in high stress/anxiety mode when they go into these doctor's offices, they can be accidentally conditioned to stress out when they are exposed to fish tanks in other settings.[66]

Scientists have conducted follow-up research that is even more mind-boggling. Even *unrelated thoughts* can get linked to a traumatic event. For example, if you are thinking about pizza just before a bad car crash, every time you sit down to enjoy a slice of pizza, it can conjure up memories of that traumatic event.

Nick knows this firsthand. In 1967 he inadvertently found himself in the epic Baja 1000, considered to be the most grueling off-road race in North America. Motorcycles, dune buggies, and specially prepared race trucks battle the elements and each other over almost one thousand miles of desert and mountains down the Baja Peninsula of Mexico. Nick finished it on a bicycle, the first to ever do so. He didn't know there was a race planned. As part of a dare, Nick decided to pedal the length of the peninsula. He trained by riding his bicycle from the Black Hills of South Dakota to Mexico, then started down the Baja Peninsula. When he crossed the race finish line in La Paz a month after he started, all the front runners of the race were arriving. As a result, the race officials made a big deal out of it and included him in all the celebrations. Imagine, in the midst of high-tech, high-powered off-road race vehicles, Nick pedaled and pushed a Raleigh Carlton ten-speed the whole way. He could have died at several points, surviving on rancid water from mud puddles and scavenged food. As a result, he experienced nearly every gastrointestinal symptom in the book.

Today, more than fifty years later, when Nick passes a Mexican restaurant, he often instantly recalls the symptoms he experienced. Classical conditioning still links Mexican food with the traumatic memory of the putrid water he had to drink. What he experienced is a unique form of conditioning whereby a single exposure will induce his symptoms, and the trigger doesn't have to occur at the same time as the symptoms. It can be hours or even a day or more later when the symptoms appear. This conditioned form of taste aversion is called the Garcia effect and is not uncommon in cancer patients being treated with protocols that affect their gastrointestinal system.

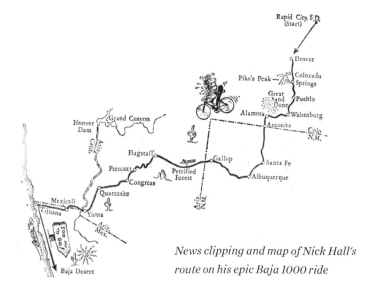

News clipping and map of Nick Hall's route on his epic Baja 1000 ride

Youth Off on 2200-Mile Bicycle Trip to Mexico

By JACK R. SIMPSON
Special to The Daily News

Well, young Nick Hall of Chicopee Falls is at it again.

This time he's off on a cycling trip from Rapid City, S.D., where he has been working at the Black Hills Reptile Gardens, 2200-miles southwest to the lower tip of the Baja peninsula.

Needless to say, Hall is a physical fitness enthusiast of the first order.

1808-Mile Cycle

And this is not his first long-distance cycling venture. It was in the fall of 1963 that he cycled from Rapid City, where he has been employed wrestling alligators and milking rattlesnaked(!), to the home of his parents, Mr. and Mrs. Maxwell L. Hall of 104 Pondview Drive in Chicopee Falls, a distance of roughly 1808 miles.

Evidently, a summer without having been "snakebit" or "crushed by alligator jaws" has prompted Hall to look for something exciting to do before registering in December at Springfield College where he will be a biology major in his second year.

And so he convinced a cooperative cycle manufacturer to sell him a special racing bike at cost (a feat in itself). Other gear, such as camping equipment, was obtained from local merchants.

He plans to average about 100 miles daily as he heads southward to Denver, Colorado Springs, Pueblo, Walsenburg, Alamosa and Antonita in Colordo, through Santa Fe, Alburquerque and Gallup in New Mexico, through Flagstaff, Prescott, Congress, Quartzsite and Yuma in Arizona, and then on to Mexicali and Tijuana in Baja.

About 300 miles below the border, as if his cycling won't provide enough adventure, he'll be met by his summer employer, Earl Brockelsby, for a 30-mile trek through desert unexplored to this day.

---

2 Flat Tires So Far

The Daily News has received word from Hall as to how he plans to return to Massachusetts. It will be by bicycle.

He writes that since he has left South Dakota his bicycle has had "two flat tires."

His first night on the road, he writes, was "spent with friends in Chadron, Neb., the next night with the Scottsbluff Fire Department, and the past three nights on the side of the road.

"I'm now in Colorado Springs and will spend two days hiking on Pike's Peak. Then I strike out for Baja and should rendezvous with Brockelsby on Oct. 17.

"Provided all goes well, I'll pedal back to Massachusetts around the end of November or the first of December."

If Hall completes his journey, he will have pedaled approximately 5,800 mlies.

Rapid City, N.D., to Baja, Mexico — 2200 miles.

"To our knowledge, no one has ever crossed this area," Brockelsby said. Hall added: "We know there are some who tried and didn't make it."

Upon return to their base camp, Hall will again board his bicycle for the remaining 500-mile trip down the peninsula.

Along the entire route he plans to sleep in police stations, jails, fire stations, missions, anywhere he can get in out of the elements.

His companion of former trips, Arbuckle, a two-foot alligator, and Sappho, a large tortoise, will not be along this trip. But since he has said that he will probably try to hunt most of his food, he will undoubtedly be busy enough without his companions.

Generally, he travels with very little cash and on this trip he expects to supplement his sparing diet with rattle snake meat from Baja. Hal became accustomed to eating rattlesnake fillets while working at the Reptile Gardens. He describes it as tasting about like "barbecued chicken."

Whatever his adventure, Hall will have tales to tell his classmates when he arrives here in December, God willing. He hasn't announced as yet how he will travel here.

Every woman who has breastfed a child knows that initially physical stimulation is required to release oxytocin to get milk letdown. However, the physical stimulation is usually preceded by the sound of their child crying because they're hungry. In short time, the sound of the crying alone can cause the milk letdown. It's a "Pavlov's mom" response, because even another child's crying will stimulate that milk letdown—embarrassing if you're sitting in a restaurant or a similar public space.

So those are some of the downsides of classical conditioning. These types of mental associations are now undisputed. Music, objects, and even aromas after sufficient pairing with a pleasant experience will acquire the ability to evoke a memory of that experience. Totally unrelated stimuli can trigger responses because the brain has learned to make an association between the two. But can classical conditioning be used to train ourselves to respond in a healthy way to stressors and triggers? Absolutely.

See how this is all coming together? Stress recovery strategies, lifestyle strategies, classical conditioning, cross-stressing, eustress. The Stress Recovery Effect is both the *means* and the *end* to a better life.

NICK HALL: IN HARM'S WAY, PART 2

When the World Trade Towers were attacked on 9/11, I called Mom to check on her, as so many others did during those dark days. She was in Massachusetts and seventy-six years old at the time. I said, "What do you think about all of this?" She said, "I don't really know what they're making such a fuss about. This is nothing compared to what the poor people in Dresden, Germany, went through during the war. We went through it for years in London. I suppose I can understand because nothing like that has ever happened in America before."

She was saying, "I survived that. Now I can handle anything."

I found that same spirit among the WWII generation at the Reptile Gardens, where I worked as a teen wrestling alligators and milking rattlesnakes. Some of them took even greater risks than I did. I don't think they thought of it as taking extreme risks. They were just super optimistic. "I survived the war. I can do these crazy things with rattlesnakes. What's the big deal?" They were my mentors who convinced me that doing those types of things was quite normal. [67]

They had experience with unusual stressors. Their bodies had trained for it because they'd experienced stress. Mom never gave up inducing eustress into her life either. She was featured in the documentary movie Young at Heart, *which highlighted the past and present endeavors of a group of elderly singers who took their passion for pop music and rock 'n roll to the streets. The documentary won major awards before becoming one of the few documentaries to be shown on the big screen as a movie. It opens with a close-up of my mother's mouth belting out "Should I Stay or Should I Go."*

Where was that spirit of optimism and resiliency forged? Well, everyone had to do something during the war years. Her job was organizing singalong songs in the bomb shelters. She dragged an old piano down into the nearby underground subway station where those in danger would seek refuge. As the bombs rained down from above, their voices echoed defiantly through the darkness.

I look back now and see that she survived by implementing stress recovery strategies. Every afternoon, she would walk with her dog, rain or shine. That was her winding-down ritual. Inherently, she knew the value of the Stress Recovery Effect.

I was the next generation. I didn't go through the war, but my mother's attitude was, "You live each day to the hilt because you may not be alive tomorrow." So, at fourteen, when I wanted to hop on a Greyhound Bus near my home in Massachusetts and go out to South Dakota and play with poisonous snakes, she was like, "Fine. Do it. If that's what you want to do, go and do it."

I guess it helps explain why I'm the way I am, because she was very happy-go-lucky too. She didn't really plan things. She just went with the flow, somehow figuring that it was all going to work out. She knew that by giving me the freedom to experience repeated encounters with stressors and danger, my body and brain would build resiliency for any dark days ahead.

Later she told me she was scared to death when I was out there, but she wasn't going to let me know that. She said, "You've got to get out there and have these experiences and take risks," and I did. I still do. Recently I completed another unsupported bicycle ride that began in Seattle and ended six weeks and over three thousand miles later in Tampa, Florida. I guess I'm a product of my upbringing!

Today I'm the one who is scared to death when my children and grandchildren are pushing the limits. But I'm not going to let them know that. I'm just glad they're out there too.

CHAPTER 6 TAKEAWAYS

In Harm's Way, Part 1

Nick's mom built up unusual resiliency during the horrors of World War II. How is it that she and many others from that generation reentered a more normalized life with positive and upbeat attitudes while others succumbed to fear and anxiety?

After 1945

How do the rest of us build up similar resiliency to the stressors we face today? Scientifically based techniques can train the body and brain to recover automatically from distress. We can be trained to *manage what you can control*. You have a chance to inject positive eustress into your life in a way that strengthens your whole being so you can handle more distress and spend more time in the Optimal Zone.

Injecting Eustress

By intentionally and repeatedly injecting eustress into your life, the Stress Recovery Effect brings maximum benefits. Eustress can and should be injected into our lives in three different ways.

1. **Physically Induced Eustress**. Physical exercise is one of the most effective ways to train your body and brain to recover quickly from stressors. Almost any form of exercise will work as long as it significantly increases your heart rate and you can do it in cycles called intervals.

2. **Mentally Induced Eustress**. You can use mental exercises to train your body and brain to be more resilient and recover faster from stressors. These exercises might include board games or competitive internet social challenges.

3. **Emotionally Induced Eustress**. Intentionally exposing yourself to things you consider fearful is a great way to train your body how to recover from stress and to overcome those fears.

The Science Behind It

The amazing intricacies of the brain can be leveraged through classical conditioning, stress recovery strategies, and lifestyle strategies. The Stress Recovery Effect is both the means and the end to a better life.

In Harm's Way, Part 2

Life is dependent on us pushing our bodies, stretching our minds, and facing our fears. Our experiences with stressors can train us to be better. In a peaceful modern world, it's important that we expose ourselves to regular doses of eustress. It's important that we get out there and do it.

"Life begins at the end of your comfort zone."
—NEALE DONALD WALSCH

CHAPTER 7

LIFE IN THE PITS

*Going Slower to Go Faster with
the Stress Recovery Effect*

DICK TIBBITS: REAL LIFE, PART 1

I was a counselor at the time. When I met Mary,[68] I could see it on her face. She had come to me with the stated intention of wanting to be a better mom, but the lines on her face and the desperation in her eyes told a deeper story. In my office her full story eventually tumbled out in tears, frustration, and shame.

Mary was an unpretentious and dedicated mother. Her dependability in fulfilling the many responsibilities she cheerfully accepted endeared her to many. Her warmth and smile were contagious.

Bob, Mary's husband, was likable enough, but she felt he was irresponsible in many ways. Bob would take things as they came and didn't worry much or plan ahead. Many half-finished jobs lay around the house, and he could never be counted on to get things done.

This pattern of irresponsibility bothered Mary. She'd cry, and he'd be baffled by her tears. "Why does she get so upset?" he would ask. Mary wanted stability and long-term planning. Bob, on the other hand, appeared to be a little boy in an adult body. He saw no reason to take life as seriously as Mary.

Eventually Mary came to realize that by shouldering most of the responsibility in the marriage, she had become more like Bob's mother than his wife. She resented Bob for this, and he, in turn, avoided her to escape her "nagging," as he called it.

Steadily their conflicts intensified as the years went by. The peaceful days they shared in the beginning of their marriage seemed to come further and further apart. Aggressive quarrels became the norm, followed by days of silent withdrawal. There were attempts at reconciliation and promises to try harder, but all too often their conflicts would arise again and the resolutions to do better would be crushed under the pressure of what appeared to be ever-increasing irreconcilable differences.

The birth of their child, Robbie, had not brought them together as they hoped it would. Mary had subconsciously believed the baby would draw Bob closer to her, hoping Bob would become more responsible because of the care required by the baby. Instead, just the opposite happened. Mary had more responsibility while Bob took less. Their backgrounds, lifestyles, and values were so different they seemed unable to agree on anything. Despite this, Bob and Mary would not give up hope on achieving a workable marriage. They remained committed. They had been raised in the church, and both were convinced divorce was wrong.

One night during a terrible quarrel, Robbie came out of

his room rubbing his sleepy eyes and pleading through his tears, "Please, Mommy and Daddy, don't fight anymore. Don't you like each other?"

Shocked into rationality by the simple words of their son, Bob and Mary faced the fact that they did not like each other anymore. Neither would choose the other as a friend. How could they go on pretending to be husband and wife? And now they faced the reality they had tried to deny before: Their conflicts were deeply affecting their son.

That's when Mary came into my office for counseling. The tension and pain on her face revealed the four-year struggle with chronic mental, emotional, and physical stressors. The desperation in her eyes betrayed the acute fear from the tearful pleadings of her son.

It was a turning point for the marriage.

PIT STOP

Like Mary and Bob, real life bombards all of us with relentless stressors. Motorcycles and alligators are intense examples of triggers, and they make for great stories. But it's the everyday stressors that get to us most often. What about your story? What stressors do you experience day to day in your life? The principles and strategies we have shown you work in all situations wherever your stress response is triggered. It might involve the breakup of a relationship, the loss of a child, financial insecurity, or concerns about appearances.

Athletes make for exciting examples, but athletes only have to perform at their peak for a short period of time. Of course, they still have personal issues to deal with during the off season. The teacher, parent, or corporate leader has to perform at high levels continually. Compared to an athlete, your stress is equally as extreme—and possibly more so—because it goes on relentlessly without a break.

The Stress Response Strategies we shared with you in the previous chapter are designed to help you during acute short-term threats. And that's good. But as we know all too well, bad results occur when the stress response doesn't shut off. Maybe it's the nagging concern that your weight continues to creep slowly upward. Will the kids be okay when they go off to college? What will the neighbors think if you're driving an old car? These are valid concerns that can trigger your stress response in situations that don't benefit from your stress responses at all. This toxic cycle of chronic stressors can lead to behaviors that cause more stress responses. It's a cycle, and it's hard to tell what got it started. Are you running away because you're stressed? Or are you stressed because you're running away? Does the trigger cause the stress response, or does the stress response become the trigger? As is so often the case, both are true.

When most people think of motorsports, they think of the action on the track—motorcycles flying high, cars hitting walls, smoking tires, and the winner's circle. Yes, it's a good show on the track, and that's what pays the bills. But the pits are where the most important action takes place. It's what happens *behind* the scenes that makes peak performance possible on the track. The pits are where the mechanics and technicians work meticulously, where the team captains choreograph the pit crews and pit stops, where the racers rest, take on nourishment, and get their heads ready to race.

You also need to manage what goes on in your "pits" so you can better manage what happens out there in real life. Doing so will open new horizons for you. But it won't happen when you're stuck in rush-hour traffic trying to get your kids to band practice. It won't happen in the moment when you get blindsided with criticism during the PTA meeting. You need to come into the pits. You need to train. You need a strategy. You need a plan.

GETTING MAXIMUM LEVERAGE FROM THE STRESS RECOVERY EFFECT

The Stress Recovery Effect exercises we recommend will train you to recover faster. If you train properly *now*, stressors will automatically trigger a propensity to recover *later*. And it's so simple: *By repeatedly training your brain and body with eustress, the stress response can be conditioned to trigger recovery from stressors of all kinds.*

Here's how:

- ⊙ Exercise physically, mentally, or emotionally.

- ⊙ Get your heart rate to climb to a target level.

- ⊙ Slow down to bring your heart rate back down.

- ⊙ Do it again and again.

Memorize this simple formula:
Exercise. Recover. Repeat.

A MATTER OF THE HEART

The easiest way to measure the intensity of an exercise is by monitoring your heart rate. Up to this point, we've been trying to help you get your heart rate down. Now we're going to ask you to strategically increase it—just like an athlete intentionally trains hard.[69]

The heart rate we are most interested in is around 80 percent of your maximum heart rate.

There are two easy ways to measure heart rate.

1.   While you're exercising, if you are unable to speak comfortably, then you're probably exercising close to 80 percent of your maximum heart rate. If you can converse with ease, you are probably below that level, closer to 60 percent. Use your ability to speak to gauge your exercise level. Then vary the intensity so it feels as though you are balancing the more intense episodes, during which you have difficulty speaking, with equal and opposite intervals when you can converse with ease. That gives you the simple "exercise, recover, repeat" experience you want.

2.   If you use a heart rate monitor, keeping track of your heart rate is easy. For the average person, the simple wrist monitor is effective. For the athlete

who's pushing it to the nth degree, a more accurate chest strap monitor is recommended.

To know when you're at 80 percent of maximum heart rate, you must know what your maximum heart rate is. Let us give you ballpark generalizations here, but please know that your numbers will be unique.

Most people can approximate their maximum heart rate by subtracting their age from 220. Therefore, if you are forty, your estimated maximum heart rate will be 180 beats per minute (220 − 40 = 180). The chart below will save you time trying to calculate your maximum heart rate (MHR).

AGE	ESTIMATED MHR (220 MINUS AGE)	80% MHR	60% MHR
20	200	160	120
30	190	152	114
40	180	144	108
50	170	136	102
60	160	128	96
70	150	120	90
80	140	112	84
90	130	104	78

A short word of caution about heart rate monitors. Heart rate monitors are great at measuring your stress response. However, they can also trigger a stress response for some people. In one study in the 1980s, Nick put heart rate monitors on cancer patients who were participating in a guided-imagery study. He wanted to measure how well they were relaxing. So when their heart rates went up, it was because they thought they were going to disappoint the researchers by not relaxing properly, and that concern became a stressor that increased heart rate. In this case, use of the monitors increased their anxiety and made it harder for them to relax properly. That could potentially happen to you if your stress response is triggered when a "beep" or number on your screen causes you to worry for any reason. Be kind to yourself and, with practice, this concern should go away.

Intervals

The most common cardiac exercises expend energy for a fixed amount of time, or perhaps over a certain distance. Invariably, a person exercises at the same intensity and then at the end slows down and stops. The end represents the start of the recovery phase. Most people get thirty or more minutes of stressing their body by placing additional demands on it, but just a single recovery period at the end. Yet it's recovery they need to learn. We all get plenty of experience with stress, but not with recovery.

How do you create more of this important recovery phase while exercising physically, mentally, and emotionally? By oscillating with intervals, a simple workout strategy that works.

Intervals simply raise and lower your stressors multiple times. By repeatedly exposing yourself to stress and recovery, you can train yourself to recover quickly and efficiently. The goal is to intentionally increase heart rate as part of a controlled cycle. When heart rate goes up and you've reached a target number of beats per minute, you slow down and allow your heart rate to come down. And then you do it again and again. Exercise. Recover. Repeat.

- ⊙ If your high heart rate (HR) is 120, then come down to 80 before starting the next interval.

- ⊙ If your high HR is 140, then come down to 100 before starting the next interval.

- ⊙ If your high HR is 160, then come down to 120 before starting the next interval.

- ⊙ Build the intensity of the workout until your heart rate reaches about 80% of your maximum.

- ⊙ A drop of 40 BPM is a good transition rate for interval training.

- ⊙ Repeat about four times, eventually working up to six interval cycles.

Why these numbers? Because for every action there needs to be an equal and opposite reaction. It doesn't have to be an exact number. *What is important is that each burst of increased exercise is followed by a comparable amount of recovery.* Please remember that these are approximate numbers. The intensity of the workout, your thoughts, room temperature, food intake, and many other factors can shift the intensity up or down. The actual heart rate numbers are different for everybody.

It's all about making sure the amount of stress is

comparable to the amount of recovery. Stressing your body causes the beats per minute (BPM) to go up. Recovery takes place as heart rate comes down. Stress, recovery, stress, recovery with every cycle.

Faster Recovery with Interval Training

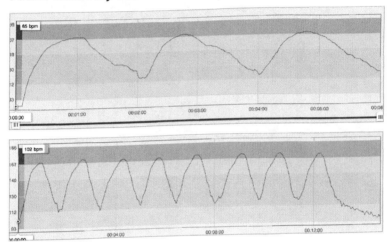

Here is a good example of what we're talking about. The first graph is an interval session with a racer Dick worked with when he first began to practice intervals. Notice how long it took to bring his heart rate down. The graph looks like a gentle slope, indicating that it's taking longer to recover. Now look at the next graph. Notice how much faster recovery occurs. The steeper the slope, the quicker the heart rate comes down. Now these results did not happen overnight. This took many weeks of practice. But today this athlete can go from a heart rate of 170 down to 120 in less than 30 seconds. That is rapid recovery. He has achieved a remarkable balance between stress and recovery, and because of this he's capable of handling more intense stress because he will recover more quickly.

With practice, you'll be able to improve your recovery time too. Thanks to classical conditioning, the increased BPM eventually becomes the trigger for recovery. If you train right, stressors will automatically trigger a propensity to recover.

Counterintuitive? Maybe. But you now know why this works! It's simple. If Dick's wife had gone back to Busch Gardens regularly and gotten back on the coaster multiple times, her heart rate would not have climbed as high as it did. She could have reduced her fear of roller coasters by normalizing the experience and using the principles outlined in this book. She would have also trained her brain and body to recover faster from any stressor. Of course, this assumes she wanted to learn to enjoy a good roller coaster ride.

Polar Plunges and Other Intervals

Physical exercise intervals are the most obvious choice for training your body and brain to recover. But that's not the only kind. The mental and emotional exercises we unveiled in the last chapter work too. Essentially, anything that raises your heart rate in repetition is going to train your brain and body in the same way.

Nick recently visited two Scandinavian doctor friends in Minnesota. It was early spring, and the scenery was stunning. They had a beautiful log cabin on a lake with a sauna. Everyone got well heated in the sauna before the doctors said, "Okay, come follow us." They marched Nick and the other guests down to the edge of the lake—which, of course, was still rimmed with ice. Then the two doctors dove off the dock into the lake. One by one each of the guests followed suit.

The ice-cold water took Nick's breath away. But then he felt amazingly refreshed and invigorated. Among other more typical treatments, these two doctors recommend this type of intense interval to improve health. What it's doing is forcing your blood vessels to suddenly dilate to release heat when you get hot in the sauna, and then rapidly constrict to prevent losing any extra heat when you hit the cold water. It's a form of interval training, especially if you repeat the process several times. Try running cold water over your body after a hot shower. It will prepare you to meet the stressors of the day.

This type of training helps the sympathetic and parasympathetic nervous systems to do what they're supposed to do. And this training strengthens and automates the process of stress recovery. It's not about simply training your heart to recover; it's about training recovery from stressors. Some of the same brain chemistry that controls heart rate impacts your reaction time, memory, dietary choices, sleep, and mood, as well as a host of other physiological and mental events associated with stress-induced emotions.

By implementing interval training for your body and mind, your body will learn to expect recovery and start doing it automatically when your heart rate (stress response level) begins to rise. For you, a rise in heart rate during the exercise part will become the equivalent of Pavlov's bell. Recovery will eventually become an automatic response to stress.

STARING DOWN THE DRAGON

Polar plunges and other intense physical, mental, and emotional eustressors are all great triggers for interval training. But what do you do if there's a trigger that causes undue distress, and it's a trigger you can't avoid? Sometimes our fears seem like a massive fire-breathing dragon prowling in the dark ready to devour us.

This is where we get into the realm of phobias. Phobias are intensely felt fears that can cripple us and seriously hinder us from living productive lives. Brave as we might try to be, taking down this dragon can seem impossible. But it's not.

Some years back, Dick worked with a top-ranked Supercross motorcycle racer—one of the guys who does jumps that launch them thirty feet into the air while at racing speed. Dick saw that he had the potential to be a national champion.

But there was one problem. His sport required random drug testing. Whenever his name was selected, he became so anxious that it affected his race results in a negative way. He got tense and tight, slowing his speed and increasing small physical and mental mistakes. His heart rate jumped prematurely. Sweaty palms. Short, tight breaths. This problem had to be solved if he was going to be number one. What triggered this fearful response? Was he afraid of getting caught using drugs? No, he was clean as a whistle when it came to that.

Through talking with him, Dick learned that the racer's fear was rooted in a traumatic accident in his past. Tucked away in his memory was the impact of pain, the blare of sirens, the bloody chaos in the ER—and, in that context, the painful injection of needles. It was the needle that was triggering the detrimental stress response during drug testing. Dick knew that he would need to gradually bring this racer face-to-face with his fears. For if the fear of the needle continued to paralyze him, his racing career would be seriously compromised—perhaps the rest of his life too.

To address the rider's anxieties, Dick had him come to the hospital to draw blood. At first, they just walked by the lab. They discussed topics that interested him, and that relaxed him a little. Next, they walked into the waiting room and then walked out. After doing this a couple of times they took a seat in the waiting area, then walked around. Each time they took one step closer to the lab—and then backed away to safety. As he got used to each successive step, he remained in control of how far he would go and when he would walk away. The process became easier for him. Finally, he was in a chair having his blood drawn without any significant stress responses.

The end result: a successful career. A life free from that fear.

For the treatment of stress-provoking fears, we use what is called *progressive approximation*. If someone has a fear of something, we move them toward it. When they encounter it, then we move them away from it. Then we move them toward it again. When they get comfortable with a certain level, we then move them a little closer. Repeatedly, the emotional fear is heightened and then dialed back. Eventually the intermediate steps give a sense of control and mastery. The next step forward can be taken more easily. With each approach, the emotional response is elevated, followed by the feeling of gaining control. You can see the cycles of stress and recovery, even in this exercise. It's the same principle used in interval training only it uses emotional stress. You can overcome major phobias this way. The control factor is important here. You are the one who controls how you move toward the stressor that triggers your fears. You are the one who chooses to back away from the trigger.

The advantages of this type of interval training go far beyond what the heart can measure. But you must take small steps. Baby steps if necessary. Slowly you will feel comfortable leaving your familiar surroundings and operating with a new set of beliefs.

What is your "dragon" today? Examine each emotion you experience along with your beliefs about it. Then, by immersing yourself in situations you typically avoid, you can gain the confidence necessary to attempt new behaviors. Armed with these new skills, you'll be able to stare down the dragons in ways you never imagined possible.

Fear comes from the inability to predict. You think "that roller coaster could kill me" or "that needle could take me out." But after enough exposures where nothing bad happens, you gain the ability to predict that nothing bad *is going to* happen. If you've never experienced it, however, you don't have the data stored in your brain that nothing bad is going to happen to you, and you are living off the anticipation of the unknown.

Herein lies the solution to fears: When fears and uncertainties occur, turn to the familiar. Using successive approximation, you can turn the fearful unfamiliar into the familiar. It never hurts to do this in the company of family or close friends. The more familiar a person or place is, the more likely you can predict what it's going to be like, and this too will give you more confidence to stare down the dragon.

The Science Behind It: Cross-Stressing

Dolphins can be trained to do remarkable things, and so can we. When working for the Office of Naval Research, Nick's job was training bottlenose dolphins as part of a stress-related communication study. Their task was to press an underwater paddle when they heard a certain sound. When they were first placed into the tank, the animals were clueless. They didn't know where they were or what they were supposed to be doing. The training was done in gradual stages.

At the start of their training, the dolphins would be touched gently with a handheld paddle as they swam around the side of the tank. A fish would be tossed in a dolphin's path the moment the touch was applied. Eventually the dolphin made an association between touching the paddle and getting fed. After that, the paddle was attached to an underwater apparatus that the dolphin would swim to on its own, press, and be fed.

As the animal started moving toward the paddle, a sound would play. Next, only when the animal pressed the paddle *after* hearing the sound would it be fed. Then the frequency and intensity of the sound would be adjusted, and eventually the dolphin learned to respond only to a specific sound before it received a reward. That was the ultimate objective: to teach the animals to discriminate between different auditory signals.

Learning this simple task took the dolphins several days. But once the animals had acquired what was called a learning set, Nick could substitute other sounds or use visual cues and the animals would figure out the problem in a fraction of the original time.

This is the important part: Dolphins don't just learn. Dolphins learn to learn. People learn to learn too. Even cells can learn to learn. It is well documented that if the concentration of a chemical increases within the body, there will be a corresponding adjustment in the ability of the receptor to attract the chemical. It's one of the ways the body adapts to change. The concept of learning to recover from one form of stress to better manage other forms is something Nick refers to as *cross-stressing*.

The Plan

Strategic use of successive approximation and cross-stressing can completely turn the tables in our battles with stress. Lots of people endure stress. However, few take the time to teach themselves to recover from the stress response. Most don't even know that it is possible! Events giving rise to stress may well be outside your control, but recovery is in your hands.

After you've done intervals a few times, your body will anticipate recovery and start doing it automatically when your heart rate begins to rise. If you do your training right, it doesn't take much time—and you might truly enjoy it! You're not taking something away from your schedule; you are adding something that will add to your life in all aspects.

How? You can turbocharge the results with Lifestyle Strategies and Response Strategies by putting to use all the tools you learned in Part 2. It's time to pull them out of the toolbox and put them to excellent use! Combine them and you have the secret sauce that turbocharges the Stress Recovery Effect.

THE STRESS RECOVERY EFFECT ACTION PLAN

We've summarized the most important action points from this book into an Action Plan. The plan is simple, doable, and within your control. The Action Plan helps you practically incorporate the Response Strategies and Lifestyle Strategies into your daily routine. Use this tool to begin new habits of stress recovery for a lifetime of success. You can find it on page 326. Make copies of the pages and follow the plan for at least the next four to six weeks.

Don't let the simplicity of the plan fool you. As with all types of learning, repetition makes it work. You are training your brain and body to make healthy, positive changes. After you've done the Action Plan on a regular basis, your body will learn to expect recovery and start doing it automatically. You'll also begin to train yourself to automatically use Lifestyle Strategies and Response Strategies in the right places. Recovery will eventually become automatic!

DICK TIBBITS: REAL LIFE, PART 2

"Please, Mommy and Daddy, don't fight anymore. Don't you like each other?" Those words from her three-year-old son still haunted Mary when she first came into my counseling office, her face and heart heavy under the weight of the stressors she was shouldering.

She was ready to work on the marriage. Her husband, Bob, reluctantly agreed to start counseling to try to restore the relationship. Mary tried, but it soon became clear that Bob was indifferent. He wasn't willing to change, and he stopped attending after a few sessions.

As their marital problems grew in intensity, Bob gradually dropped out of activities at church. He said he felt like a hypocrite to go to church in the morning only to engage in a furious argument with Mary later in the evening over some trivial matter. Eventually they both stopped attending church because Mary was too embarrassed to go by herself.

In time, Bob decided to end their problems by filing for divorce. Mary's problems, however, were only going to intensify. Mary felt like she had endured a hurricane of relational turmoil; now the personal tidal wave of divorce crushed her. The stressors of having to pay the bills, being a single mother of a young child, and having no one who seemed to care or support her was overwhelming. Frightened and embarrassed, guilt weighed heavily upon her as she could not escape the feeling of failure on her part. After all, she felt she could have been a better wife—and if she had been, maybe she would not be alone now.

Emotionally, she was withdrawing. She withdrew from the support of her church because she felt like she had failed to live up to her standards as a Christian. She had an overwhelming sense of being alone and abandoned. Nobody understood. She didn't understand. Her world was falling apart; she thought there was nothing she could do about it. In my mind, I pictured her trying to hold on to the edge of a cliff but slipping off and falling into space: No place to land. No place to get her feet on the ground. Feeling like she was totally out of control.

Somehow Mary found the strength and courage to join a Stress Recovery program I was leading. But it was not easy. Fear of rejection kept her from opening up in the group. She came to me and asked for advice, listing many of the issues she was struggling with. Gently, I said, "The real issue is your withdrawal and isolation. Being in a group gives you a chance to help yourself. If you share in a group, it gives us permission to support you, to ask questions, and lets others in the group in. It's time to begin breaking through. You have allowed the divorce and your husband to turn you into a victim. Until you take control and start to change that, there is no way out."

Over the next few weeks, she began to open up, using the Stress Recovery seminar presented by the authors as a place to share her struggles. She learned how to frame her circumstance and what to do when she felt emotionally overwhelmed. She bought a simple heart rate monitor and realized her heart rate was still way too high. By practicing Recovery Strategies, she saw her heart rates stabilize when she was bombarded with stressors. She saw for the first time that she was able to control something in her life that she felt was out of control. Soon she could talk about her divorce and pain without choking up and getting emotionally overwhelmed. Other breakthroughs started to happen as she brought her stress response down to a functional level.

By slowly and consistently implementing Lifestyle Strategies, Mary was able to see her life in a new light. She had learned to manage what she could control and to release what she couldn't. She had learned to go slower to go faster. Stressors that previously overwhelmed her she now saw as challenges, and she knew how to manage them. I watched as her confidence and warm smile returned. I watched as she did her best with her son and began to serve others again.

Today her life is far from perfect. Real life never is. But by learning to take control of what we can, people like Mary— and people like you and me—can do more than just survive. We can thrive.

CHAPTER 7 TAKEAWAYS

Dick Tibbits: Real Life, Part 1

The story of Mary and Bob is true. The stressors they experienced in their marriage were real and intensifying when they came to Dick for counseling. Real life for each of us is relentless in the challenges it puts us through. Our destiny is largely determined by how we respond.

Pit Stop

Normal life bombards us with continual stressors, whether we are an alligator wrestler, motorcycle racer, parent, spouse, student, or just working hard to keep the bills paid. In this race of life, we need to pull into the pits where we can work behind the scenes to coordinate a healthier, more vibrant way of living.

Getting Maximum Leverage from the Stress Recovery Effect

By repeatedly training your brain and body with eustress, the stress response can be conditioned to trigger recovery from stressors of all kinds.

This is done by:

Exercise. Recover. Repeat.

A Matter of the Heart

Heart rate is the easiest way to measure the intensity of an exercise or stressor. The simplest way to measure heart rate while exercising is to speak. If you can speak comfortably, you are probably at less than 80 percent of your maximum heart rate. If you can't speak easily, you're probably above 80 percent. Heart rate monitors can be very helpful to accurately measure heart rate.

Intervals

Repeating the "exercise, recover, repeat" routine trains your body to recover from stressors more effectively and quickly. Intervals inject repeated doses of eustress into your life routine. The goal is to intentionally increase heart rate as part of a controlled cycle. Polar plunges and other types of intervals, including mental and emotional exercises, train the body and brain to recover from stressors of all kinds.

Staring Down the Dragon

Successive approximation can break the fear behind our phobias and give healing and freedom from past stressors. By taking steps toward the stressors that frighten us, backing off in a controlled way, and then taking steps even closer, we can condition ourselves to calmly face situations that once terrified us.

The Science Behind It: Cross-Stressing

Animals and humans can learn to do amazing things. We can even "learn to learn" through practice and repetition. Every cell within the cardiovascular system, respiratory system, and even the immune system has the ability to learn to recover more quickly from stressors.

The Plan

Intervals train your body to expect recovery and start doing it automatically when your heart rate begins to rise.

1. Do an exercise that induces stress either mentally, physically, or emotionally.

2. Follow up each exercise with a Response Strategy.

3. Aim for five intervals three times a week.

Dick Tibbits: Real Life, Part 2

One of the fateful differences between Mary and Bob is Mary's willingness to seek help, open up, and make changes. Life is never perfect, but Mary's story shows that we can all respond to stressors in ways that lead to a sense of control, a changed mindset, and decisions and actions that result in a healthy, fulfilled existence.

"Training gives us an outlet for suppressed energies
created by stress and thus tones the spirit just as
exercise conditions the body."
—Arnold Schwarzenegger

CHAPTER 8

LIVING ON PURPOSE

Finding New Horizons Through
Mission, Vision, and Purpose

W hen Dick works with racers, one of the first principles he teaches them is to look farther down the track and not focus on the track right in front of them. What is happening right in front is happening too fast for the brain to fully process. Thus, there is great danger of overreacting when their horizon is too short. It is simply impossible for their brain to process conditions that quickly when they are going 200 mph. Looking farther down the track smooths things out and gives them a better perspective. It also helps them to prepare now for what lies ahead rather than always reacting to what is going on right now.

Key Principle #3: Look Farther Down the Track

In many ways, this is like life. Events can come at you so quickly, it seems impossible to keep up. You find yourself reacting to each event rather than planning ahead. So how do you look farther down the track?

We suggest three approaches to improving your life:

1. Have a purpose in life that becomes a beacon toward which you are heading.

2. Have a vision for your future, and visualize how you would live life now in order to get to where you want to be.

3. Have a time frame with goals for how you get from here to there, so you have a way to track your progress.

We will unpack these three principles in this chapter. But before we go on, we want to share with you what one participant in our Stress Recovery Effect program said about her experience using the principles you have learned in this book:

I was showing signs of high blood pressure, and many people I spoke with said I showed signs of high stress, and one recommended I attend the Stress Recovery Effect program as a means of controlling it. To be fair to myself and my health, and not having had issues with stress in the past, I thought taking this class would be beneficial.

Up until now, I thought I had managed my stress well. There were certainly times I felt more stressed than others, which I figured was normal, but the results were troubling me since I've had an otherwise very healthy life. So taking this class was an opportunity for me to control and possibly eliminate this issue.

As part of taking this class, I learned that not all stress is bad. Certainly, there are some that are bad and there are methods to control the impact this stress has on your life. But there are other stresses that people take on in their life that are good, that challenge you and make your life worth living. I hadn't thought about that before and it made me realize I needed some stress, but also needed to control the bad stress and not let it impact my health.

I now recognize having some stress in life is good, to challenge yourself mentally and physically, but I also learned techniques to control the impact of bad stress in my life. I learned that how we handle stress is personal to each of us and not the same, and how to recognize those times where I'm becoming very stressful. The biggest challenge is learning how to handle those stressful moments where you can feel your blood boil and controlling how that stress impacts you. Unfortunately, you can't eliminate those moments as much as you try, but you can learn techniques to make sure this stress doesn't hinder your health. Breathing techniques, exercises, clearing your mind, and thinking clearly are all examples I've used to get me past those moments. And now it's good that I think about them ahead of time so I can be mentally prepared when those moments strike (whereas before I would just react and not realize what that stress was doing to me).

Though we may never meet in person, we've been honored to share our stories with you. It's a privilege to pass on some of the life-giving principles that have directed our lives into better places over the decades. But this book was never about us. We meant for this book to be about you. Why did you read this book, and where are you now on your life's journey? What was the "why" for you? Maybe it was serious health issues from prolonged chronic mental distress. Maybe it was the unrelenting demands from work. Maybe you are in the pressure cooker of parenting or marriage. We are confident that your initial "why" was attached to a lingering hope that perhaps some of the tensions and pressures of life could be reduced.

Let's review what we have said thus far.

Part 1 set the stage. We needed a fresh perspective so we didn't get stuck in the same old approaches:

Chapter 1 explored **definitions**.

- ⊙ **"Stress"** is a tension or pressure between two things. Some of the different kinds of stress include physical, psychological, and spiritual.

- ⊙ **"Stressors"** cause the stress. The intensity and impact of stressors is highly relative to the situation and the person.

- ⊙ **"Triggers"** are input from the five senses to the brain, as well as thoughts and memories already in the brain.

- ⊙ **"Interpretation"** is the highly complex mental analysis of triggers.

- ⊙ **"Stress responses"** react to the brain's interpretation.

Chapter 2 illuminated **The Good, the Bad, and the Ugly** faces of stressors.

We introduced a fresh paradigm showing how the stressors that trigger our stress responses can be divided into three different continuums:

- ⊙ Eustress and Distress

- ⊙ Physical and Mental

- ⊙ Chronic and Acute

Then we confessed that all this is not as black and white as we seem to make it. Nothing in the human body and brain is black and white because of the incredible complexity of the body and neurological systems. The difference between "eustressors" and "distressors," for example, is highly dependent on the person and the situation. Physical and mental stressors are so intertwined that you have to consider them as one. We were clear, however, about "The Ugly" long-term mental distressors and the psychosomatic problems that can kill us when the stress response system gets left in the "on" position.

Chapter 3 was about **The Optimal Zone** and how there is an optimal range of intensity for any given stressor, for any given person, in any given situation, at any given time. We also explained how your inner brain stem, middle diencephalon, and outer cortex can all work together to manage stressors through conscious decisions and metacognition. The bottom line for finding serenity and balance was Key Principle #1:

"Manage what you can control."

Part 2 equipped you with the fourteen strategic tools you can use to build a better life.

Chapter 4 unveiled **Response Strategies**, the seven actions you can take to get immediate help *in the moment.*

1. **Breathe It Out:** Responding to Stressors One Breath at a Time

2. **Stretch It:** Flexing to Avoid Snapping

3. **Let It Go:** Tensing Up to Wind Down

4. **Act It Out:** Do It to Feel It

5. **Pause It:** Buying Time for Better Choices

6. **Rock It:** Swaying Away the Stressors

7. **Laugh It Up:** Laughter Is Still the Best Medicine

Chapter 5 was all about **Lifestyle Strategies**, the seven long-term strategies that will drastically improve stress *over the long haul.*

1. **Think About It:** Engaging Your Outer Brain for the Better

2. **Sense It:** Creating Environmental Eustress

3. **Reduce It:** Cutting Stressors Off at the Source

4. **Forgive It:** Finding Freedom from the Past

5. **Move It:** Exercise Always Wins the Day

6. **Eat It Up:** Ingesting the Good Stuff

7. **Give It a Rest:** Taking Intentional Breaks for Ultimate Performance

In Part 3, we've been learning to use those tools. Applying powerful mental and physical strategies, we have learned how to train the brain and body in ways that maximize the Stress Recovery Effect.

You've learned a lot, and our hope is you are already applying much of the information. If you've been drowning in stressors, we know these principles are already allowing you to tread water and keep your head above the surface. What now? How do we wrap this up? Let us ask a probing question:

Is it possible this last chapter is really just the beginning of something new?

We think so. It's time to think beyond your initial *why* and think bigger, further, and deeper. We invite you to look farther down the track. Up to this point this book has been about you, and we are pleased that you're not drowning in stressors anymore. Why? Because it is difficult to think about anything else when you're sinking below the surface. But now your head is up. And we want you to do more than just *survive*. Because we believe you can *thrive*.

NEW HORIZONS

So far we have mentioned two types of stressors: acute and chronic. But there is a third type that can be just as devastating. It's called existential anxiety. This is when you are concerned that there are forces at play, way beyond your control, that impact you. For example, when will the button be pushed that sets off a nuclear holocaust? Have I wasted my life, and if so, to whom will I be accountable for that? Is there life after death, and if there is, will I be a part of it?

Many of us experienced this during the COVID-19 pandemic. We were anxious and stressed by the extreme disruptions to everyday life. First responders were heroic when placed in situations they had never faced before. But you could also see the stress in their eyes and hear it in their voices. A stress was there that we all felt went way beyond our ability to control.

And yet, even in this rapidly deteriorating environment, people responded in positive ways. Volunteers went out to get much-needed groceries and supplies for the elderly, families did takeout to help local restaurants survive, and people kept their distance from each other to break the rapid spread of this virus. Despite all the stress, people responded in many helpful ways, which in turn helped them better manage their own stress.

To survive, we need to manage what we can control. To thrive, we must move beyond to the factors we *can't* control at all—things like COVID-19—that threaten our very lives and the lives of those we care about. In the big picture of life, there are few things we can control. Is there anything I can do to keep my country from financial collapse? Can I stop billions of people from gobbling up natural resources? What kind of a world will our children inherit?

The media, of course, keeps distressing news in front of

us because it sells. The bad news keeps us revved up, burned out, and ultimately depleted and paying attention during the commercials so we will buy things we didn't need in the first place. But in the end, there's not much we can do about most of these bigger issues.

Keep in mind that life is more than rising above our problems and reducing stressors. As humans, we can do much more than simply function according to predetermined genetic programming; we are wired to have a purpose and find meaning in what we do and how we live. What do we do with the issues we clearly can't control or predict? We either *deny* them or *trust* in something bigger than ourselves. Denial never plays out well. Trust is different. To find trust in its most powerful form, we need to look beyond the physical and explore the spiritual.

Our purpose, and what we do with our lives, is ultimately a spiritual journey. Spirituality has many definitions, but the unifying theme of all spiritual practices is to give our lives context.

- ⊙ Context arises from your connection with self, with others, and with a higher level of purpose in life beyond mere existence.

- ⊙ Context tells us where we have been, where we are, and where we are headed.

- ⊙ Context is the bigger picture that makes the snapshots of life make sense.

In the spiritual journey we develop our personal value system, our sense of social responsibility toward others, and our search for meaning in life. For many, spirituality takes the form of religious observance, prayer, meditation, and a belief in God. But again, one size does not fit all, as spirituality finds its expression in different ways for different people.

Nick is heavily involved with Rotary International. His spiritual journey is guided by Rotary's Four-Way Test:

Of the things we think, say, or do:

1. *Is it the TRUTH?*

2. *Is it FAIR to all concerned?*

3. *Will it build GOODWILL and BETTER FRIENDSHIPS?*

4. *Will it be BENEFICIAL to all concerned?*

Dick's spirituality took root in the Adventist tradition. In his work for AdventHealth, he finds his mission for healing the whole person: body, mind, and spirit. Having a spiritual context frames everything else in life.

One way that many people do this is through prayer. In times of deepest distress, people often turn to prayer to seek help and guidance in their lives. Prayer is a tangible way of reaching outside yourself and recognizing that someone bigger than yourself cares and is there to help you. Such a practice can reduce your stress by giving you a readily available way to talk about your concerns to someone you believe takes a real interest in your life. We encourage people to make their prayers: Personal – Simple – Direct.

CULTIVATING SPIRITUALITY

Let's unpack the three approaches to improving your life that we discussed at the beginning of the chapter.

1. Bring a Sense of Purpose

Cultivating your spirituality will help you access what is most meaningful in your life. By clarifying what really matters in life, you can focus less on all the other issues that daily disrupt it and that, if left unchecked, can build over time to become chronic stressors. This process of prioritization about what is important in your life reduces the number of issues you need to worry about. If everything is equal, then nothing is a priority, and you are left chasing the last stressor that disrupted your life. People with a strong sense of purpose deal more effectively with life's disruptions because they see them in a broader context. They have their priorities straight and thus concerns can be weighted from most important to least important. Difficulties become tests of character rather than insurmountable roadblocks.

2. Have a Vision for Something Bigger Than Yourself

The more you feel you have a purpose in the world, the less alone you feel and the more connected you become with others who share your worldview. This can provide you with inner peace during difficult times. It also helps to give perspective about what are truly the important things in life and what is simply clutter and noise that surrounds us. When you feel a part of something greater, you realize you aren't responsible for everything that happens around you or to you. Spiritual people don't perceive themselves as simply a product of their environment; rather, spiritual people see themselves in the context of something larger or more significant. Because of this, they can rise above their current circumstances.

3. Have a Time Frame for How You Get from Here to There

Stressors can become overwhelming when you get caught up in everything life can throw your way. The consequence of such a life is that you work harder and faster and either get nowhere or, worse, get further behind. No matter how hard you try or how fast you run, you never get anywhere.

But for the spiritual person this is not true. When you step back and look at the bigger picture, you can begin to see your direction in life and your progress along the way. It may be slower than you'd like, but you are on a path to get from where you are toward where you want to be. You know there will be setbacks along the way but they are only temporary, for you have a purpose in life along with a clear vision of where you want your life to be. So you can now recognize that with each day, you are getting closer to your goal.

With this higher perspective, it will be easier to access the Optimal Zone and make more informed decisions that keep life on track and in harmony with a higher purpose.

We live in an era of tremendous scientific advancement. We can be very thankful for the knowledge that has allowed us a peek into the marvelous complexity of the human brain. We should stand in awe of the design of the human body, the beauty of the physical, and the complexity of your brain's mental processes. We know so much more than we did, and yet, humbly, we acknowledge that we continually stand on the threshold of eternal mysteries.

BEYOND OURSELVES

Spirituality means looking *beyond* ourselves for meaning and purpose; this connects us to something profoundly more impactful than anything we can achieve on our own. Ironically, when we begin to experience it, we discover that the most precious elements of life are given to *us* when we give to *others*. Don't ask us how this works exactly. It's totally counterintuitive. We instinctively try to *get*, but it turns out we get when we *give*.

True giving starts with altruism. Altruism makes the world a better place; it helps both the receiver and the giver, thus doubling your investment. It's doing something beyond myself that doesn't necessarily *directly* benefit me. Except it does. People who give do get something directly in return. They get better health, reduced stress, and an inner sense of calm and joy. These conclusions are well documented in Ken Pelletier's book *Sound Mind, Sound Body: A New Model for Lifelong Health.*[70] In it, Dr. Pelletier comes to this powerful conclusion: "Lifelong good health is far more dependent on a positive, purposeful life orientation than on aerobic workouts and regimented low-fat diets."

Altruism happens when people look beyond themselves to care for someone else right where they are. Think of a boy mowing the lawn of the widow next door. Think of a woman who gives up an evening to sit with a grieving friend. Think of a girl sorting cans at the food bank. Think of first responders entering a community after a hurricane. Think of a student putting his body between a gun and his friends. Think about the civil rights movement and marching into Montgomery, Alabama. You can do that if you embrace altruism and a purpose—a *higher* purpose.

Altruism has tremendous health benefits, increasing our resilience to stressors and providing a surge of "feel good" neurochemicals.

- I'm turning something I can't control into something I can control.

- I find purpose and expectation in the future because my life has meaning beyond my life.

- Helping others pushes me beyond my comfort zones.

- Being involved in something larger than myself often leads me into new relationships and bonding experiences.

When we live our lives altruistically, we trigger all the good feelings we want for ourselves. It's almost as if we were *designed* for this altruistic kind of life.

Key Principle #4: Life Is Best When We Live for
Something Beyond Ourselves.

Keep the altruism principle in mind as we move beyond ourselves and step toward these new horizons.

MY BIGGER PICTURE

Life is short. We get one shot at making it count. Unmanaged stressors rob you of precious time and resources when you are doing your best to invest in a meaningful life. Spiritual development makes the difference between moving through your days with direction or wandering aimlessly. To further understand your spiritual self, take time to answer these questions:

- ⊙ Who are the people who bring richness to your life?

- ⊙ What do you value most in life?

- ⊙ Where do you get a sense of community and feel like you belong?

- ⊙ What inspires you and gives you hope?

- ⊙ What is a cause beyond yourself that could push you toward new horizons?

Your answers will help you identify your most important people and experiences. That, in turn, will help you discover and develop a purpose/vision statement.

Dick's personal mission statement is: *"To add value to everything I do by not only improving outcomes but enriching the lives of those around me."* When Dick retired, he got stuck for a moment while he tried to figure out what to do for the rest of his life. He knew he had to reinvent himself. But he didn't reinvent himself totally or just roll the dice and make some guess. He took thoughtful inventory of his experiences, his resources, and his passions. He knew he wanted to give back, and he wanted to stay young while working with kids. Then he went out and found opportunities to do it through performance coaching for young athletes in motorsports and executive coaching for rising stars in the corporate world.

Nick processes his mission from a different standpoint. He feels his life is driven by his *thoughtful reflection* on his life circumstances. He defines success as *"making progress toward a worthwhile goal."* When he finds himself in a particular situation, he reflects on it and then creates a purpose and vision in response to that situation. When something happens to him, he thinks, *What purpose can I turn this into? How can I use this experience to do something differently? What if I keep doing the same thing?*

For example, Nick never planned to ride bicycles across the country to raise money to eradicate polio. It wasn't until someone in his Rotary Club said he should combine his love for bicycling with the cause of polio. Now that has become one of his passions and purposes. He doesn't have a developed, preexisting purpose statement. He looks for an *opportunity*, assigns it a purpose, then does something about it. A recent purpose is to create adventuresome opportunities similar to his own for the emerging generation of young people. He's now serving as Scoutmaster of a Boy Scout troop and introducing them to WaterTribe adventures and cross-country cycling.

You don't have to guess which one of us is the administrator and which is the adventurist! These are two different approaches to experiencing meaningful purpose in life. Which one of us does it the right way? Once again, the answer is, both of us. Both approaches are completely valid. Yet each approach has its limitations and dangers. That's why the two of us need each other as friends. We bring balance to each other.

Think about it! Take a five-minute break. Better yet, when you take your next day off, keep all the above questions in mind. Let your answers gel. Then write down your own purpose and mission statement. Don't make it complicated. Just ask yourself what difference you want to make in the world and for those immediately around you. Post it somewhere you will see it regularly. You can use your life mission as an anchoring point to make any necessary adjustments to your life. Doing so provides an inner calm to know your life is on track and heading in the direction you want it to go. With this information, you can focus your search for spirituality on the relationships and activities in life that have helped define you as a person and those that continue to inspire your personal growth.

WHERE AM I HEADED?

Goal setting will help you fulfill your mission and vision. Mission and vision statements are usually grand, expansive, and nebulous. Goals are more specific and reflect what you need to do. In this way, goal setting produces healthy eustress. If you want to become a better athlete, you'll need to push yourself physically. If your goal is to be a nurse, you need to learn to be comfortable with blood, odors, and sticking people with needles.

Goals create a new tension between where you are and where you want to be. It's not distress, because what you want to do has a purpose. And that's different from stressors that simply happen to you. This is intentional. This is part of the plan. Your goals make the mission tangible. Objectives are a subset of your goals. If your goals are big, you'll need to break them down into a to-do list.

What are the actions you need to take today to start your spiritual journey? What do you need to do this week, this month, this year? Get started by making a list of your goals and supporting activities.

- ⊙ Things I need to do today

- ⊙ Things I need to do this week

- ⊙ Things I need to do this month

- ⊙ Things I need to do this year

END GAME

Today is the first day of the rest of your life. You have new tools to transform your stressors from enemies to allies. All the information you've learned in this book has been grounded in science and experience. No matter what, we are challenging you to go for it, because your days here are going to come to an end, one way or the other, sooner or later. It's not a matter of *if*, but *when*. May God give you the optimism of an adventurist and the wisdom of an administrator. Hopefully you'll find a dynamic balance between both and then pursue life to the fullest.

We believe the strategies in this book will serve you well for the rest of your life. Now it's up to you to put them into practice. You have the tools to be successful; we simply want to encourage you to use them as often as you need to. Take back control over your life so you can live the abundant life you were meant to.

Remember:

- ⊙ Harnessing stress requires some thinking and doing.

- ⊙ One size never fits all.

- ⊙ One formula never fixes everything.

- ⊙ It's going to take choices.

- ⊙ It's going to take action.

And it's going to be worth it.

No matter where you are in the journey, all lives begin with what you choose to achieve today. Don't worry about how far away your goal seems to be. What's truly important in life is the journey, and you will never achieve your heart's desire unless you are on that journey today. Do you want that full and meaningful life you deserve? Then get started today and you will get there.

CHAPTER 8 TAKEAWAYS

New Horizons

To survive, we need to manage what we can control. To thrive, we must move beyond to the factors we *can't* control. What we do with our lives is ultimately a spiritual journey. Spirituality has many definitions, but the unifying theme of all spiritual practices is to give our lives context:

- ⊙ A sense of purpose
- ⊙ A vision for the future
- ⊙ Looking farther down the track

Beyond Ourselves

Spirituality means looking *beyond* ourselves for meaning and purpose that connect us to something profoundly more impactful than anything we can achieve on our own. Spirituality leads to altruism, which has amazing benefits for the giver as well.

My Bigger Picture

To further understand your spiritual self, take time to answer important questions about your personal passions, dreams, goals, and objectives. Then develop a personal mission statement to tie it all together.

Where Am I Headed?

Create goals that fulfill your mission.

What Do I Do to Get There?

If your goals are big, break them down into objectives—a to-do list.

End Game

Life is more than dealing with all the challenges that lie in front of you. Chasing after every issue that presents itself in your life will lead to what many call the rat race. Life was meant to be more than endless challenges and setbacks. Life was meant to be lived, and lived to the fullest. So accept our challenge to go for it, because so many wonderful possibilities exist in your future. Live life without regret. Live the life you were meant to live. It's your life, so live it!

Now that you've discovered the benefits of learning how to recover from stress, it's time to embark on an action plan and begin to apply these principles to your daily life. Research supports taking immediate action on an idea to ensure its success. That's where the Stress Recovery Effect Action Plan comes into play. We recommend you follow the Action Plan a minimum of 4-6 weeks, but to really ingrain these principles as habits, do it for up to 12 weeks.

On the opposite page (and in the bonus online materials), you will find a card titled "The 7 Stress Response Strategies." You will want to keep these near at hand as a reminder to practice them. Here are some ideas: photocopy the page, cut out the card and post it where you will see it regularly. You can also download it, print it, and cut it out. In addition, take a photo of the card with your smartphone, crop it, and save it on your phone, tablet, or computer. Keep it where you can refer to it frequently. This will help remind you to use the Stress Response Strategies whenever you're experiencing distress in the moment.

The Stress Recovery Effect Weekly Planner begins on page 328. You can also access the Planner in the bonus online materials. Again, you can photocopy or download these pages. This section helps you apply the Lifestyle Strategies—the longer-term strategies that help prevent you from experiencing distress in the first place. A section for practicing Interval Training with eustressors is on page 329, and another section for journaling your stress recovery begins on page 330.

We wish you great success as you apply the principles of *The Stress Recovery Effect*!

STRESS RECOVERY STRATEGIES

Make copies of this page, cut out the cards, and place them in locations that will remind you to use the Response Strategies whenever you're experiencing distress. Response Strategies are *intervention* tools that you can use immediately when you're facing high acute stressors. You may review them in chapter 4.

THE 7 STRESS RESPONSE STRATEGIES

1. **Breathe It Out:** Responding to Stressors One Breath at a Time

2. **Stretch It:** Flexing to Avoid Snapping

3. **Let It Go:** Tensing Up to Wind Down

4. **Act It Out:** Do It to Feel It

5. **Pause It:** Buying Time for Better Choices

6. **Rock It:** Swaying Away the Stressors

7. **Laugh It Up:** Laughter Is Still the Best Medicine

© *The Stress Recovery Effect*, Hall & Tibbits, AdventHealth Press

Week #   Starting Date:

RESPONSE STRATEGIES

I have placed the cards with the seven Response Strategies in places I will likely see them when I'm facing distress (page 138). I will refer to them and practice them throughout this week.

LIFESTYLE STRATEGIES

Choose one or two Lifestyle Strategies to focus on this week. Lifestyle Strategies are *prevention* tools that will keep you from the extremes of distress when they occur.

1. **Think About It:** Engaging Your Outer Brain for the Better (page 179)

2. **Sense It:** Creating Environmental Eustress (page 189)

3. **Reduce It:** Cutting Stressors Off at the Source (page 195)

4. **Forgive It:** Finding Freedom from the Past (page 201)

5. **Move It:** Exercise Always Wins the Day (page 212)

6. **Eat It Up:** Ingesting the Good Stuff (page 217)

7. **Give It a Rest:** Taking Intentional Breaks for Ultimate Performance (page 228)

Write down how you will incorporate the Lifestyle Strategies you have chosen into your life this week. Be specific.

_____

_____

_____

_____

_____

Write down the specific lifestyle goals you want to reach by implementing the strategy you have chosen.

1. Lifestyle Goal: _____

_____

2. Lifestyle Goal: _____

_____

STRESS RECOVERY INTERVAL TRAINING

Pick a self-induced mental, emotional, or physical eustressor that you will use this week for your interval training and describe it below (pages 258 and 288).

_____

_____

_____

_____

Choose one of the Response Strategies below to use after each time you induce the eustressor you have chosen for this week. Repeat with five intervals each time. Practice this Eustressor/Recovery Strategy routine at least five days this week.

1. **Breathe It Out:** Responding to Stressors One Breath at a Time (page 143)

2. **Stretch It:** Flexing to Avoid Snapping (page 148)

3. **Let It Go:** Tensing Up to Wind Down (page 151)

4. **Act It Out:** Do It to Feel It (page 157)

5. **Pause It:** Buying Time for Better Choices (page 162)

6. **Rock It:** Swaying Away the Stressors (page 167)

7. **Laugh It Up:** Laughter Is Still the Best Medicine (page 170)

Check off your progress each time you complete an interval training:

JOURNALING YOUR STRESS RECOVERY

Using a notebook, journal, or writing software, take at least a half hour this week to answer the following questions as they relate to stress recovery. You may choose to write your thoughts in one thirty-minute session or five minutes daily.

Too Little Stress

In what areas of life am I experiencing too little stress (i.e., boredom, fatigue, frustration, or dissatisfaction)?

_____

_____

_____

_____

What positive actions can I take to challenge myself to grow in these areas?

_____

_____

_____

_____

Optimum Stress

In what areas of life am I experiencing optimum stress (i.e., creativity, progress, satisfaction, or performance improvement)?

_____

_____

_____

_____

What can I do to maintain, protect, and enhance those areas?

_____

_____

_____

_____

Too Much Stress

In what areas of life am I experiencing too much stress (i.e., exhaustion, illness, feeling overwhelmed, or inability to concentrate)?

_____

_____

_____

_____

Describe any experience that triggered stress symptoms this week.

_____

_____

_____

_____

Describe which strategies worked well to recover from stress and how I used them.

_____

_____

_____

_____

What actions can I take to use Response and Lifestyle Strategies in the week ahead? Be specific.

_____

_____

_____

_____

Additional Notes

....

_____

_____

_____

_____

_____

ACKNOWLEDGMENTS

Nick Hall

First and foremost, I thank my loving wife Hazel for more than 50 years of support and encouragement while keeping the home fires burning during my cross-country cycling and kayaking adventures. Those undertakings continue to serve as the testing grounds for stress-recovery techniques. My daughters, Rachele and Stephanie, along with my grandchildren, Jackson, James, Abigail, Chase, Brian, and Jack have become adventure-seekers in their own right. That's made me realize that worrying about the safety and well-being of loved ones eclipses all other stressors.

In particular, I'm deeply indebted to the many people who have encouraged me over the years: Sir Norman Snow, my biological father who I never knew but whose influence was conveyed through my mother's recollections of his resourcefulness and heroism during WWII. There was always a glimmer of hope that I might have inherited one of his genes. My mother, Eileen, who after having survived the London Blitz in 1940 taught me to live each day to the hilt in case it was my last, but to do so responsibly in case it wasn't. Maxwell Hall, my stepfather, who taught me the value of hard work and altruism. Earl Brockelsby, the owner of the Black Hills Reptile Gardens, who instilled a passion for adventure and risk-taking when he hired me to wrestle alligators and milk rattlesnakes at his tourist attraction in South Dakota. More recently, Steve Isaac, the founder of WaterTribe's arduous, human-powered boat challenges through the Florida Everglades.

Jim Czarnowski and his associates at Hobie Cat, for their generous support in making their tough boats and equipment available for these demanding events. Finally, Jim Loehr, my colleague and friend whose work with professional athletes led to his recognition of the need to balance stress with recovery in order to achieve the ideal performance state.

Dick Tibbits

There are many people who touch your life, and if you are lucky and blessed, some will have a profound impact on your life. I would like to thank those people who made writing this book possible for me.

First, I want to thank my wife Arta for the stability and joy she has brought to my life. I also want to thank Des Cummings, Jr. for his creativity and the opportunities he provided me to create programs such as *The Stress Recovery Effect* program we launched at Florida Hospital—today Advent Health. And of course, Todd Chobotar for his paving the path for me to get published not only for this book, but for several others.

It was a great opportunity for me to work with many of the world's best motorcycle racers and help them to remain calm under pressure. At such a young age, very high expectations are placed on them to perform. If they don't learn how to manage this stress, it will work against them, and there will be another young rider waiting in the wings for their chance to excel. I would like to thank two factory team owners in particular: Roger DeCoster with team Suzuki and

Gary Gray with Indian Motorcycles. These men had a vision that high-performance racing was more than simply having the fastest bike. The rider also needed to be finetuned to perform at their best.

And I got to work with some very fast riders. I worked with Kevin Windham in Supercross, and in my favorite sport of American Flat Track, I had the privilege of working with such stars as Jared Mees, Nichole Cheza Mees, Briar Bauman, Sammy Halbert, and Brandon Robinson. They were all winners in my book.

Finally, there were the thousands of participants who went through *The Stress Recovery Effect* program. Their feedback helped make the ideas of this book real. For the principles of this book are not only for the elite athlete, but for everyone who faces stress that can be overwhelming and who needs tools and insights in how best to recover and move on.

ABOUT THE AUTHORS

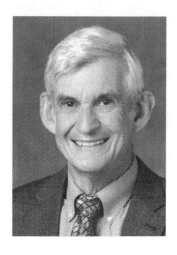

Nick Hall, PhD, is a medical scientist and the recipient of an honorary MD. Since 1979, Nick has conducted groundbreaking studies linking the mind and body. This research has been featured by national and international media, including CBS's *60 Minutes*, the BBC's *Nova* series, and the Emmy Award–winning program *Healing and the Mind*. He is the recipient of two prestigious Research Scientist Development Awards from the National Institutes of Health and is the author of the best-selling audio series *I Know What to Do, So Why Don't I Do It*, published by Nightingale-Conant. In addition to his academic pursuits, Nick is no stranger to the more pragmatic aspects of how emotions impact health. After earning his way through college wrestling alligators and milking rattlesnakes, he worked as an intelligence operative for the US government. He also led a *National Geographic*–sponsored expedition to the West Indies, where he studied mass-stranding behavior in whales. At his Saddlebrook Resort headquarters, where since 1998 he has directed the Wellness Center, Dr. Hall creates team building and wellness programs for some of America's leading corporations and athletes.

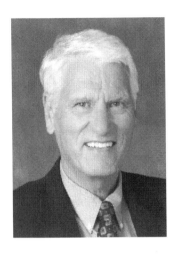

Dick Tibbits, DMin, has a doctoral degree in psychotherapy from Andover-Newton in Boston. Dick is an ordained minister, a licensed professional mental health counselor, a clinical pastoral educator, and a hospital administrator. As a hospital administrator, he has been a VP for both Operations and Human Resources, as well as a COO and CEO. Currently Dick is a performance coach to some of the world's premier motorsports racers. During his career, Dick pastored in New England, then became an educator and hospital administrator at Kettering Medical Center, Florida Hospital (now AdventHealth) Orlando, Loma Linda University Medical Center, and Florida Hospital (now AdventHealth) Tampa. Dick conducted original research on forgiveness and heart disease, which he presented at the National Institutes of Health, Harvard University, Mayo Clinic, Duke University, Loma Linda University, and Stanford University. He was a featured speaker at the International Conference on Stress and is the author of *Forgive to Live: How Forgiveness Can Save Your Life*, currently printed in eight languages. His latest work on *The Stress Recovery Effect* is written from his wealth of experience working with those who must perform in extreme stress situations.

ENDNOTES

1   Simon Sinek, *Start with Why: How Great Leaders Inspire Everyone to Take Action* (London, England: Penguin Business, 2019).

2   Milja Milenkovic, "42 Worrying Workplace Stress Statistics," The American Institute of Stress, September 25, 2019, https://www.stress.org/42-worrying-workplace-stress-statistics.

3   Richard S. Lazarus, *Emotion and Adaptation* (New York: Oxford University Press, 1991).

4   Leon Festinger, "Cognitive Dissonance." *Scientific American* 207, no. 4 (1962): 93–106. https://doi.org/10.1038/scientificamerican1062-93.

5   Leon Festinger, *A Theory of Cognitive Dissonance* (California: Stanford University Press, 1957).

6   Blaise Pascal, *Pensees (Thoughts)* (Boston, MA: MobileReference.com, 2010).

7   C. Hellingman, "Newton's Third Law Revisited," *Physics Education* 27, no. 2 (1992): 112–115, https://doi.org/10.1088/0031-9120/27/2/011.

8   "Average Duration of a Single Eye Blink," Average duration of a single eye blink – Human Homo sapiens—BNID 100706, accessed August 12, 2020, https://bionumbers.hms.harvard.edu/bionumber.aspx?id=100706.

9   For an excellent review of the subject of stress and how it impacts the body, see Robert M. Sapolsky, *Why Zebras Don't Get Ulcers: A Guide to Stress, Stress-Related Diseases, and Coping* (New York: W.H. Freeman and Co, 2004).

10   Howard S. Friedman and Stephanie Booth-Kewley, "Personality, Type A Behavior, and Coronary Heart Disease: The Role of Emotional Expression," *Journal of Personality and Social Psychology* 53, no. 4 (1987): 783–792, https://doi.org/10.1037/0022-3514.53.4.783.

11   Lydia Temoshok, "Personality, Coping Style, Emotion and Cancer: Towards an Integrative Model," *Cancer Surveys* 6 (1957): 545–67.

12   "Eustress," Merriam-Webster.com, accessed August 25, 2021, https://www.merriam-webster.com/dictionary/eustress.

13   "Types of Stressors, Eustress vs. Distress," MentalHelp.net, accessed August 25, 2021, https://www.mentalhelp.net/articles/types-of-stressors-eustress-vs-distress/.

14   María J. Leone et al., "The Tell-Tale Heart: Heart Rate Fluctuations
       Index Objective and Subjective Events during a Game of Chess,"
       Frontiers in Human Neuroscience 6 (2012), https://doi.org/10.3389/
       fnhum.2012.00273.

15   L.M. Jaremka, C.P. Fagundes, J. Peng, J.M. Bennett, R. Glaser, W.B.
       Malarkey, and J.Kv Kiecolt-Glaser, "Loneliness Promotes Inflammation
       During Acute Stress," *Psychological Science* (in press).

16   A.C. Phillips, D. Carroll, V.E. Bums, C. Ring, J. Macleod, and M. Drayson,
       "Bereavement and Marriage Are Associated with Antibody Response to
       Influenza Vaccination in the Elderly," *Brain, Behavior, and Immunity* 20,
       no. 3 (2006): 279–289.

17   J. K. Kiecolt-Glaser, L. Fisher, P. Ogrocki, J. Stout, C. Speicher, and R.
       Glaser, "Marital Quality, Marital Disruption, and Immune Function,"
       Psychosomatic Medicine 49, no. 1 (1987): 13–34.

18   Robert M. Yerkes and John D. Dodson, "The Relation of Strength of
       Stimulus to Rapidity of Habit-Formation," *Journal of Comparative
       Neurology and Psychology* 18, no. 5 (1908): 459–482, https://doi.
       org/10.1002/cne.920180503.

19   Cynthia D. Fisher, "Boredom at Work: A Neglected Concept,"
       Human Relations 46, no. 3 (1993): 395–417, https://doi.
       org/10.1177/001872679304600305.

20   Sheldon Cohen, "Keynote Presentation at the Eighth International
       Congress of Behavioral Medicine Mainz, Germany, August 25–28, 2004,"
       International Journal of Behavioral Medicine 12, no. 3 (2005): 123–131,
       https://doi.org/10.1207/s15327558ijbm1203.

21   Roman M. Wittig, et al., "Social Support Reduces Stress Hormone Levels
       in Wild Chimpanzees across Stressful Events and Everyday Affiliations,"
       Nature Communications 7, no. 1 (January 2016), https://doi.org/10.1038/
       ncomms13361.

22   Letitia Anne Peplau and Daniel Perlman, *Loneliness: A Sourcebook of
       Current Theory, Research, and Therapy* (New York: Wiley, 1982), 1–18.

23   Amanda J. Rose and Karen D. Rudolph, "A Review of Sex Differences in
       Peer Relationship Processes: Potential Trade-Offs for the Emotional and
       Behavioral Development of Girls and Boys," *Psychological Bulletin* 132,
       no. 1 (2006): 98–131, https://doi.org/10.1037/0033-2909.132.1.98.

24   Angela Roddenberry and Kimberly Renk, "Locus of Control and Self-
       Efficacy: Potential Mediators of Stress, Illness, and Utilization of Health
       Services in College Students," *Child Psychiatry & Human Development* 41,
       no. 4 (May 2010): 353–370, https://doi.org/10.1007/s10578-010-0173-6.

25   Suzanne M. Miller, "Predictability and Human Stress: Toward a
      Clarification of Evidence and Theory," *Advances in Experimental Social
      Psychology, Volume 14*, 1981, 203–256, https://doi.org/10.1016/s0065-
      2601(08)60373-1.

26   Martin E. P. Seligman, *Learned Optimism* (New York, NY: Pocket Books,
      1998).

27   Susan Folkman and Judith Tedlie Moskowitz, "Stress, Positive Emotion,
      and Coping," *Current Directions in Psychological Science* 9, no. 4 (2000):
      115–118, https://doi.org/10.1111/1467-8721.00073.

28   Letitia Anne Peplau, et al., "Time Alone in Daily Experience: Loneliness
      or Renewal?" in *Loneliness: A Sourcebook of Current Theory, Research,
      and Therapy* (New York, NY: Wiley, 1982), 41–53.

29   Robert M. Sapolsky, *Why Zebras Don't Get Ulcers: The Acclaimed Guide
      to Stress, Stress-Related Diseases, and Coping* (New York, NY: Henry Holt
      and Co., 2004).

30   Sheryl Sandberg and Adam Grant, *Option B: Facing Adversity, Building
      Resilience, and Finding Joy* (New York: Alfred A. Knopf, 2017), 13.

31   Ibid.

32   Ibid, 111.

33   George Fink, A. Steptoe, and L. Poole, "Control and Stress," in *Stress:
      Concepts, Cognition, Emotion and Behavior* (London, UK: Academic
      Press, an imprint of Elsevier, 2016), 73–80.

34   Sandberg and Grant, *Option B*, 111.

35   Harvard Health Publishing, "Exercising to Relax," Harvard Health,
      accessed August 13, 2020, https://www.health.harvard.edu/staying-
      healthy/exercising-to-relax.

36   Anne Cawthorn and Peter A. Mackereth, "Progressive Muscle
      Relaxation: A Remarkable Tool for Therapists and Patients," *Integrative
      Hypnotherapy: Complementary Approaches in Clinical Care* (Edinburgh:
      Churchill Livingstone, 2010), 82–96.

37   "Stress Management: Doing Progressive Muscle Relaxation," Stress
      Management: Doing Progressive Muscle Relaxation | Michigan Medicine,
      accessed August 13, 2020, https://www.uofmhealth.org/health-library/
      uz2225.

38   "Woman Fires at Cop, Virus Stress Is Cited," *Tampa Bay Times*, April 2,
      2020.

39   T. J. Berndt, "Exploring the Effects of Friendship Quality on Social
     Development," in *The Company They Keep: Friendship in Childhood and
     Adolescence*, ed. William M. Bukowski, Andrew F. Newcomb, and Willard
     W. Hartup (Cambridge, MA: Cambridge University Press, 1998), 346-
     365.

40   A helpful resource for understanding how anger and heart disease are
     linked is found in the book *Anger Kills* by Redford Williams MD 1993.

41   Dick Tibbits, *Forgive to Live: How Forgiveness Can Save Your Life*
     (Nashvillle, TN: Integrity, 2006).

42   "Dictionary.com," Dictionary.com, accessed August 13, 2020, http://
     www.dictionary.com/.

43   Jamie Pope and Steven Nizielski, *Nutrition for a Changing World* (New
     York: W.H. Freeman, Macmillan Learning, 2019).

44   M. F. Dallman, "Chronic Stress and Obesity: A New View of 'Comfort
     Food,'" *Proceedings of the National Academy of Sciences* 100, no. 20
     (2003): 11696–11701, https://doi.org/10.1073/pnas.1934666100.

45   Richard J. Wurtman and Judith J. Wurtman, "Carbohydrates and
     Depression," *Scientific American* 260, no. 1 (Jan. 1989): 68-75,
     https://doi.org/10.1038/scientificamerican0189-68.

46   Richard J. Wurtman and Judith J. Wurtman, "Carbohydrate Craving,
     Obesity and Brain Serotonin," *Appetite* 7 (1986): 99–103, https://doi.
     org/10.1016/s0195-6663(86)80055-1.

47   Nicole M. Avena, Pedro Rada, and Bartley G. Hoebel, "Evidence for
     Sugar Addiction: Behavioral and Neurochemical Effects of Intermittent,
     Excessive Sugar Intake," *Neuroscience & Biobehavioral Reviews* 32, no. 1
     (2008): 20–39, https://doi.org/10.1016/j.neubiorev.2007.04.019.

48   J. D. Fernstrom and R. J. Wurtman, "Brain Serotonin Content:
     Physiological Dependence on Plasma Tryptophan Levels," *Science*
     173, no. 3992 (September 1971): 149–152, https://doi.org/10.1126/
     science.173.3992.149.

49   Yasmine Aridi, Jacqueline Walker, and Olivia Wright, "The Association
     between the Mediterranean Dietary Pattern and Cognitive Health:
     A Systematic Review," *Nutrients* 9, no. 7 (2017): 1–23, https://doi.
     org/10.3390/nu9070674.

50   Hana Kahleova, Susan Levin, and Neal Barnard, "Cardio-Metabolic
     Benefits of Plant-Based Diets," *Nutrients* 9, no. 8 (September 2017):
     848–861, https://doi.org/10.3390/nu9080848.

51   Claire T. Mcevoy, Norman Temple, and Jayne V. Woodside, "Vegetarian Diets, Low-Meat Diets and Health: a Review," *Public Health Nutrition* 15, no. 12 (March 2012): 2287–2294, https://doi.org/10.1017/s1368980012000936.

52   Amy R. Lane, Joseph W. Duke, and Anthony C. Hackney, "Influence of Dietary Carbohydrate Intake on the Free Testosterone: Cortisol Ratio Responses to Short-Term Intensive Exercise Training," *European Journal of Applied Physiology* 108, no. 6 (2009): 1125–1131, https://doi.org/10.1007/s00421-009-1220-5.

53   M.J. McAllister et al., "Exogenous Carbohydrate Reduces Cortisol Response from Combined Mental and Physical Stress," *International Journal of Sports Medicine* 37, no. 14 (December 2016): 1159–1165, https://doi.org/10.1055/s-0042-113467.

54   Richard J. Wurtman, "Dietary Treatments That Affect Brain Neurotransmitters: Effects on Calorie and Nutrient Intake," *Annals of the New York Academy of Sciences* 499, no. 1 (June 1987): 179–190, https://doi.org/10.1111/j.1749-6632.1987.tb36209.x.

55   Do Hoon Kim et al., "Inhibition of Stress-Induced Plasma Corticosterone Levels by Ginsenosides in Mice," *NeuroReport* 9, no. 10 (1998): 2261–2264, https://doi.org/10.1097/00001756-199807130-00021.

56   N. Hall, "Alternative Medicine and the Immune System," in *Psychoneuroimmunology*, ed. Robert Ader, David L. Felten, and Nicholas Cohen (San Diego: Academic Press, 2001), 161-171.

57   P. Meerlo et al., "Sleep Restriction Alters the Hypothalamic-Pituitary-Adrenal Response to Stress," *Journal of Neuroendocrinology* 14, no. 5 (July 2002): 397–402, https://doi.org/10.1046/j.0007-1331.2002.00790.x.

58   Harvey R. Colten and Bruce M. Altevogt, *Sleep Disorders and Sleep Deprivation: An Unmet Public Health Problem* (Washington, DC: Institute of Medicine, 2006).

59   M. G. Figueiro, B. Wood, B. Plitnick, and M. S. Rea, "The Impact of Light from Computer Monitors on Melatonin Levels in College Students," *Neuroendocrinology Letters* 32, no. (2011): 158–163.

60   L. A. Pohorecky, "Biphasic Action of Ethanol," *Biobehavioral Reviews* 1, no. 4 (1977): 231–240, https://doi.org/10.1016/0147-7552(77)90025-0.

61   Detailed information on these sleep strategies and many more can be found in the curriculum *The Rest of Your Life: End Exhaustion, Enhance Energy, Sleep Smarter!* (Altamonte Springs, FL: AdventHealth Press,

2017)

62   "Loma Linda, California," Blue Zones, August 16, 2019, http://www. bluezones.com/exploration/loma-linda-california/.

63   N. Hall, M. O'Grady, and D. Calandra, "Transformation of Personality and the Immune System," *Advances* 10 (1994): 7–15.

64   James E. Loehr, *The New Toughness Training for Sports: Mental, Emotional, and Physical Conditioning from One of the World's Premier Sports Psychologists* (New York: Penguin, 1995).

65   Larry Cahill and James L. McGaugh, "Mechanisms of Emotional Arousal and Lasting Declarative Memory," *Trends in Neurosciences* 21, no. 7 (1998): 294–299, https://doi.org/10.1016/s0166-2236(97)01214-9.

66   Thomas G. Burish et al., "Conditioned Side Effects Induced by Cancer Chemotherapy: Prevention through Behavioral Treatment," *Journal of Consulting and Clinical Psychology* 55, no. 1 (1987): 42–48, https://doi. org/10.1037/0022-006x.55.1.42.

67   For a fascinating history of World War II, Reptile Gardens, and Nick's part in it, see Sam Hurst, *Rattlesnake Under His Hat: The Life and Times of Earl Brockelsby*, Vantage Point Press, 2016.

68   Names have been changed in this story.

69   Remember, before starting any exercise routine it is best to check with your physician to be sure you are safe to do so.

70   Kenneth R. Pelletier, *Sound Mind, Sound Body: A New Model for Lifelong Health* (New York, NY: Simon & Schuster, 1995).

INDEX

LIVE MORE
Happy

SCIENTIFICALLY PROVEN WAYS
TO LIFT YOUR MOOD AND YOUR LIFE

Dr Darren Morton

EXPANDED & REVISED

FORGIVE TO LIVE

HOW FORGIVENESS
CAN SAVE YOUR LIFE

DR. DICK TIBBITS